* RECIPES FOR TIME-LIMITED COOKS WHO WANT QUICK AND NUTRITIOUS MEALS.

* COOKING TIME IS 10 MINUTES OR LESS.

* THE MAIN INGREDIENT IN ALL RECIPES ARE <u>FRESH VEGETABLES.</u>

* ALL RECIPES ARE ENTREÉS. THE SOUPS AND SALADS ARE HEARTY ENOUGH FOR A COMPLETE MEAL.

* NO-NONSENSE RECIPES. ALL INGREDIENTS ARE COMMON ITEMS.

* <u>MINIMAL USE OF PROCESSED FOODS.</u>

THE 10-MINUTE

VEGETARIAN COOK BOOK

by
Phyllis Avery

Hygeia Publishing Co.
1358 Fern Place, Vista, California 92083

THE 10-MINUTE VEGETARIAN COOK BOOK

ISBN 1-880598-74-4
Avery, Phyllis, 1936-
The 10-Minute Vegetarian Cook Book

Other books by Phyllis Avery

Stop Your Tinnitus: Causes, Preventatives, and Treatments
100 Raw Fruit & Vegetable Recipes
The Garden of Eden Raw Fruit & Vegetable Recipes

PUBLISHED BY:

HYGEIA PUBLISHING COMPANY
1358 Fern Place
Vista, California 92083

Cover designed by: Alonna L. Farrar, A. Boyd-Farrar Graphics, Vista, California
Typesetting by Kathy Horeth, Morris Productions & Services, Lakeside, California

Printed in the United States of America

TABLE OF CONTENTS

TABLE OF CONTENTS

TABLE OF CONTENTS

TABLE OF CONTENTS

TABLE OF CONTENTS

TABLE OF CONTENTS

TABLE OF CONTENTS

INTRODUCTION

A new consciousness is emerging in food preparation. Health-conscious people want light, quickly prepared, simple, yet elegant, fresh food meals. This book is designed for those people.

You may have bought this cook book thinking it would explain how to make 10-minute meals using a microwave oven or a pressure cooker. I use neither method. This book is designed to teach you to cook conservatively. I developed a way of cooking vegetables that allows food to be cooked in a relatively short time while retaining most essential vitamins and nutrients.

After eating cooked foods for fifty years, I became a Natural Hygienist for health reasons. (Natural Hygiene means the eating of raw fruits and vegetables.) I'm not a purist. Only 80% of my foods are eaten raw. I am not attempting to convince you to eat your foods raw, but to explain why you should cook your foods in much less cooking time than you probably are doing now. When I wrote this book, my major concern was to preserve the nutritional value in vegetables, not to save the cook's time.

Cooks all over the world are literally cooking their food to death. Plants are living things. The moment they are harvested they begin to die. The very life of foods are enzymes, which when food is cooked at 120°F are destroyed. (The temperature of boiling water is 212°F.) Vitamins and minerals are lost in significant amounts when food is cooked. The length of cooking time, the setting of the temperature, the amount of pressure, the presence or absence of light and/or oxygen, and the amount of chopping or shredding the food has undergone...all these factors determine the exact amount of vitamin loss. If we are to obtain the most value from food, we must stop overcooking it.

A few specific examples of how heat can reduce vitamins in certain foods will suffice to show how destructive cooking can be. Take Vitamin C, for just one example. Measurements are given in milligrams by the cup, and are derived from data supplied by the U.S. Department of Agriculture. Note: Most foods are heated to 240°F in commercial canning.

Apricots.........fresh (16)........canned (10)
Bean Sprouts.....fresh (20)........canned (9)
Blackberries.....fresh (30)........canned (17)
Pears............fresh (7)........canned (2)

Another source states that when fresh peas are cooked for only five minutes, 20 to 40 percent of their thiamine (one of the B vitamins) and 30 to 40 percent of their vitamin C is lost. Because both peas and corn are more tasty raw, my recipes call for serving them raw or warming them for not more than one minute.

Mineral loss from foods by cooking occurs by the following means:

a) Leaching: The minerals are carried out in the food's own juices, which run into the surrounding liquid. Whenever you see colored water in the boiling or steaming pan, you are witnessing mineral loss.

b) Evaporation: Minerals will "bubble out" from foods upon the application of heat. Whenever you smell cooking odors, you are smelling mineral loss.

c) Chemical Alternation: Mineral salts in foods are changed chemically by the application of heat, making them biologically unavailable to the body. Whenever you taste flat, flavorless food, you are experiencing mineral loss. That explains the reason why cooked foods are so often highly seasoned.

Health is maintained only if the human body has the full range of nutrients needed and in the proper proportions. The cooking of food not only destroys nutrients so that the full range needed is not represented, but it unbalances the nutrients that remain. When this happens the body is still "hungry" and cries for more food, regardless of the huge number of calories the diner may have consumed.

When I became a vegetarian a whole new world of foods opened up to me. I discovered the extraordinary bounty available in vegetables. It was analogous to traveling to foreign countries, and experiencing the combination and flavors of different foods.

Without the use of meat, which does at least offer variety, I had to experiment with "foreign" foods. What I discovered was a gustatory delight!

You'll soon find that I discovered okra! What a diversified food! Not only does it have a sweet-pungent flavor but a built-in sauce as well. Okra is the perfect food for soups, chowders and soufflés.

Confession of an Eggplant Lover

The eggplant recipes in this book take more than ten minutes to cook. In fact they average about 15 minutes. When I found that eggplant couldn't be cooked in ten mintes, I had two choices to make. One choice was to change the title of the book to The 15-Minute Vegetable Cook Book. But since there are only five eggplant recipes in the book, I didn't want to change the main concept of the book.

The second choice was to exclude the recipes. I'm sure that after other eggplant lovers try the recipes they will be glad I kept them in the book.

All cooks have their favorite dishes. I encourage you to experience the same delight my family does. These recipes are:

> Artichoke Hearts, Noodles & Herb Sauce
> Garbanzo Stuffed Cabbage Rolls
> Butternut Squash, Snow Peas & Celery
> Lasagna Zucchini
> Stuffed Grape Leaves
> Spaghetti & Spinach with Peppers

HOW TO USE THIS BOOK

!!!STOP!!!

This cookbook is like no other you have ever used! Read this chapter before you prepare any of the recipes.

Raw vegetables and cooked vegetables do not taste the same. Remember when you were young? You refused to eat your cooked peas and decided all peas taste terrible. But in later years you discovered raw peas and you ate them quite enjoyably. I have cooked (mostly steamed) these foods so they fall between raw and cooked and have a fresh, crunchy texture. Slight steaming of vegetables releases the glucose in them, making them more flavorful. Use a timer because the meals will not be as flavorful if you cook them beyond the recommended time. Also there are differences in flavor and texture between raw, lightly steamed, and frozen or canned food. With a worldwide food import market, many previously "in season" foods are now available year-round. The only foods that are difficult to find fresh all year-round are peas in the pod, parsnips, asparagus, corn, and brussels sprouts. Where any of these is the main ingredient in any of the dishes, I suggest you wait for its local availability before planning on that meal.

The separate ingredients MUST be prepared BEFORE you begin to cook! Cooking times are short. There is inadequate time to prepare the ingredients between each step unless you have helpers.

How To Steam Vegetables

The advantages of steaming are that vegetables can be cooked in a very short time, they keep their true colors and textures, and they retain most of their vitamins and minerals. In convential cooking, most of the nutrients are lost due to high heat and lengthy cooking. When vegetables are boiled in water, the vitamins and minerals are leached into the cooking water, which many cooks throw away.

Put 1¼ cups to 1½ cups of water into a pot. Don't use tap water. (Fluoride and/or chlorine is put in most drinking water supplies in the country, and they may get into the food. Fluoridation of water causes fluorosis [mottling of tooth enamel], mongolism in infants, kidney damage, and it interferes with enzyme, mineral and vitamin functions within the system. As for chlorine, heat will drive the chlorine gas out of the solution.) Insert a steamer. The water level should be below the cage of the steamer to keep nutrients from being lost. Cover the pot, bring the water to a boil, then look into the pot. If you can see the water boiling at the bottom of the steamer, pour a little out. Place vegetables in the steamer. If using an electric stove and the vegetable requires only 4 to 5 minutes cooking time, simply cover the pot, turn off the heat, and keep the pot on hot grill. It wastes energy to steam food over high heat. The temperature of boiling water and steam remains constant regardless. The coloration that you see in cooking water and the aroma of cooking are evidence of the escape of vitamins and minerals and the destruction of enzymes (valuable amino acids). The latter occurs once food is heated to 120 degrees F. Quick steaming will minimize nutrient losses.

Most of the recipes call for adding other vegetables after some have been steaming. Add them quickly to minimize heat loss. I use a long-handled plastic strainer to flip the added vegetables into the briefly uncovered pot. Frequent additions of more vegetables causes loss of a little water. When you are following this kind of recipe, don't put extra water in the pot in the beginning to compensate for this, as it will touch the food. Instead, keep simmering water at hand and add it as necessary to keep the vegetables from scorching.

Stoves differ widely. I'm told by others that the hot plates on my electric stove stay hot longer than theirs. I suggest you experiment with your particular stove. To maintain live steam in the pot, you may have to turn the heat back to medium for a short time after two or three minutes or just leave it on low.

Steaming time also varies with the freshness of the vegetable. For instance, cauliflower and broccoli steam quicker when a week old than when fresh.

One secret of cooking food in much less time is to slice or grate it. With large uncut pieces, the outer layers become overcooked relative to the center. Spinach cooks in 1 minute. If you were to use a glass pot for steaming, you would see how quickly it goes limp.

When simmering food, always keep a lid on the pot. Every recipe except one calls for a lid to prevent the escape of steam along with enzymes, vitamins and minerals. In certain recipes I emphasize that success requires keeping the lid on. A tip: It's not necessary to raise the lid to mix many of the soupy foods. Simply take a firm grip on the handle and hold the lid down. Gently swirl the pot without lifting it from the grate.

You will notice that processed food, where specified, is cooked for a very short time because it's already partially cooked. Frozen food has been blanched prior to packaging. In the canning process, food is heated to 212 degrees F to destroy any bacteria that might be present.

Cooking instructions for fresh or frozen peas are the same but it is not necessary to cook them; they have better flavor and texture when raw. My purpose in having you simmer them 1 minute is merely to warm them. Frozen peas merely have to be defrosted and warmed.

Zucchini, in my opinion, tastes better raw then cooked. It is often eaten raw in salads. I usually cook it about one minutes mainly to warm it.

I try to use as few utensils for preparation and cooking as possible. When the food is cooked and ready for combining, merely discard the steaming water and use the same pot as a mixing bowl.

ABOUT THE VEGETABLES AND INGREDIENTS USED IN THIS BOOK

All of the grain and legume recipes require overnight soaking in distilled water. I put asterisks after the soup and salad recipe names to forewarn the cook of this, but I have omitted them in the grain and legume chapter because the introduction to this chapter explains that and other information about preparing and cooking them.

Most root vegetables like carrots, potatoes, and beets store a lot of their vitamins and minerals in and directly under their skins. Scrub the skins well with a vegetable brush. If they are especially grimy, you can scrape the skins lightly with a knife or vegetable peeler. Although I call for peeling root vegetables, the choice is yours.

If fresh corn on the cob is not available or it's inconvenient to kernel corn, frozen corn is acceptable. (Adjust the recipe to suit, as I rarely cook corn but merely warm it for 1 minute.) The meal will not be as flavorful though, and you will be sacrificing taste and quality for convenience. One corn cob yields about 1 cup of kernels.

When a recipe calls for parsnips and they are out of season (usually July, August and September), an option would be to use rutabagas. Since rutabagas take longer to cook than parsnips, either steam them slightly longer or grate them finer.

A few of the recipes call for imitation bacon chips, a soy product with seasonings similar to the taste of bacon. The flavor is overpowering. I call for soaking the bacon chips to soften their texture and because I don't want their flavor to overwhelm that of the rest of the foods. If you have never tried imitation bacon chips, you might want to use a reduced amount in your first recipe.

I prefer to dilute the Bragg's Liquid Aminos because I don't want its flavor to dominate the meal. Empty half of a 32 ounce container into a jar and refrigerate it. Then add 4 ounces of distilled water to the remaining 16 ounces and shake.

Even though I don't call for the use of salt, you might be inclined to use it. If so, never sprinkle food with salt before you cook it as this very effectively draws the juice and minerals out of it.

Even though the food takes 10 minutes or less to <u>cook</u> this does not mean that the recipes can all be prepared quickly. The preparation time of recipes is determined by the number of ingredients, how they are prepared, and how many cooking utensils are needed. Unfortunately, some of the best tasting recipes take the longest to prepare, as with all the pie recipes.

When using the blender, some foods tend to stick to the blades and the inside of the glass container. After emptying the contents, put two tablespoons of water, or whatever liquid being used in the recipe, in the blender and give it a swirl to retrieve those vegetables then add them to the recipe.

How to Wash Spinach

The root must be cut loose from the stems so that all the sand and grit can be rinsed from the adjacent small leaves. Keep rinsing until all traces of dirt are gone. If you rinse in sink or basin rather than under running water, the leaves will float to the top and the grit will sink. Drain them in a colander. Pinch off the stems with your fingers and toss the leaves in a cloth towel. If you plan to use the spinach soon after washing it in a salad, spread it on another dry towel and place it in the refrigerator for at least a half hour to dry the leaves as dressing will not stick to wet leaves. Otherwise spread the spinach evenly on the towel, roll up the towel, and place it in an untied plastic bag in the refrigerator.

I avoid the use of paper towels for drying food because they are coated with formaldehyde. Use a clean dish towel to dry or store food (like spinach or lettuce) in.

How to Clean Vegetables

Wash fruits and vegetables thoroughly before you eat them. I use a product from Amway called LOC. There are other commercial fruit and vegetable cleaners on the market. Use two tablespoonfuls in a basin or sink of water. Wash fruits and vegetables with a vegetable brush when appropriate.   Don't leave fruit in water; wash it quickly to minimize discoloration (oxidizing). Never soak vegetables for more than a few minutes. Rinse thoroughly. Dry with a cloth towel.

I also keep a spray bottle containing a higher concentration of LOC on my sink counter for quick cleaning of single items.

How to Kernel Corn

Place a large bowl in the sink. Twist the corn kerneler over the corn cob while squeezing the kerneler tightly. When you have gone halfway down, flip the cob around, and continue to the end. Go firmly and slowly. Keep the cob pointed well into the bowl because the kerneler will snap when it reaches the end, causing the kernels to scatter. Tap the kerneler clean over the bowl. Using a paring knife and a firm downward motion, scrape the "cream" off the cob into the bowl. Be sure to do this with every cob, because the cream is the tastiest part of the corn. The added flavor is quite noticeable in the recipes.

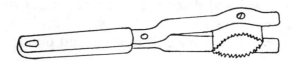

MISCELLANEOUS HOW TO'S

I prefer not to use margarine in my recipes because the oils in most margarines are hydrogenated to make them firm at room temperature. The process of hydrogenation converts polyunsaturated vegetable oil into a more solid fat by bonding molecules into long chains. In order to achieve hydrogenation economically, nickel is used as a catalyst. Unfortunately some of the metal cannot be recovered from the final product.

Coconut oil is added to some margarines and to some non-dairy cream substitutes. Coconut oil is highly saturated and may have an adverse effect on blood cholesterol. Tests have shown that atherosclerosis from cholesterol deposits occurs more in margarine-fed hogs than in hogs fed other fats.

I recommend using unrefined, cold-pressed safflower or virgin olive oil. Olive oil has been reported by the University of Texas Health Science Center to actually lower blood cholesterol.

You will notice that when I use butter for sautéing, I call for using an oil with it to prevent the butter from overheating and turning brown. (Harvey Diamond states in his book Living Health that, "It's true that butter is an animal fat, but in moderate amounts it can be handled much more easily than hydrogenated oil").

Always use cheese marked "Natural." Other cheeses could include whipped oil or consist entirely of whipped oil with flavoring.

Seasonings, Condiments & Irritating Foods

You'll notice I use very little seasoning in my recipes. Slightly cooked foods require very little seasoning because the natural taste of the food has not been cooked out. I have added many of the seasonings because most people are accustomed to highly seasoned food. Eventually you'll be able to reduce the amounts of seasoning you use.

Seasoning also increases one's appetite by creating an artificial desire for a food that is not physiologically required by the body. Overeating occurs when the appetite is artificially stimulated by seasonings. Without seasonings it is almost impossible to overeat. Seasonings induce eating long after the physiological needs of the body have been fully satisfied.

Also, many seasonings contain salt, yeast, textured proteins, artificial sweeteners, soybeans, harsh spices and herbs, MSG, fermented residues, and other deleterious substances that should never be taken into our bodies. When buying seasonings always read the label.

Drinking Water with Meals

While eating, large quantifies of digestive juices are being poured into the stomach. If water or beverages are taken, these digestive juices are diluted. The water passes out of the stomach in ten to fifteen minutes and carries the digestive juices along with it. The food is deprived of these juices and digestion is greatly retarded or stopped altogether.

In addition, drinking water and beverages leads to bolting of food. The food is washed down instead of being properly masticated and salivated. Fermentation, putrefaction, and indigestion will follow. It is recommended that you drink your water:

At least 15 minutes before meals.
At least 30 minutes after a fruit meal.
At least 2 hours after a starch meal.
At least 4 hours after a protein meal.

Eating Desserts

Desserts such as cakes, pies, puddings, ice cream, stewed fruits, etc., eaten at the end of the meal, do not combine well with vegetable or protein meals, and they cause indigestion. Also, chances are that the eater has already eaten to capacity making it unnecessary to consume more food. Desserts serve no useful purpose and are not advisable. Regarding desserts: DESERT THE DESSERTS.

Kitchen Utensils You Will Need

Electric Food Processor or Electric Food Grater
Manual Food Grater
Electric Food Blender
Manual Slicer/Grater
Electric Nut Chopper
Hand-Held Food Grater/Slicer
Digital Timer
Assortment of Sharp Kitchen Knives
Oriental Vegetable Cleaver/Chopper
Chopping Board
Corn Kerneler
Potato Peeler
Julienne Cutter (also known as a potato chipper)
Assortment of Salad Bowls
Measuring Cups (Large & Small)
Measuring Spoons

Notes

SOUP, STEWS & CHOWDER ENTRÉES

ASPARAGUS STEW

1¼ cups WATER

¾ lb ASPARAGUS, cut bite-size

4 large OKRAS, sliced

½ cup chopped RED BELL PEPPER

2 or 3 BOK CHOY stems, cut down center, thinly sliced

3 pats BUTTER or 1 tbsp VIRGIN OLIVE OIL

1 small ONION, chopped

2 tbsp BRAGG'S LIQUID AMINOS

1 large, unpeeled, chopped ZUCCHINI (need 2½ cups)

½ tsp DEHYDRATED VEGETABLE SEASONING

Steam asparagus, okras, pepper and bok choy in 1¼ cup water 4 minutes. Save water for use later.

In a 3-qt. saucepan sauté onion in butter 3 minutes.

Transfer asparagus, pepper and bok choy into saucepan. Sauté 1 minute.

Put aminos and zucchini into blender and liquefy. Add to water used for steaming and heat. Pour into saucepan. Mix. Add seasoning. Simmer 1 minute.

Ladle into soup bowls. Serve warm.

SERVES TWO

AVOCADO & CABBAGE SOUP

2 cups water

½ can CREAM OF MUSHROOM SOUP

½ cup sliced MUSHROOMS

2 cups thinly sliced, chopped
 CABBAGE (can use SAVOY CABBAGE)

3 tbsp mild, fresh SALSA

1 CORN cob, kerneled

2 medium AVOCADOS

2 tbsp minced CHIVES

Bring water to a boil in a 3-qt. saucepan. Add mushroom soup and mushrooms. Heat.

Add cabbage and simmer 4 minutes stirring occasionally. Keep covered. Add salsa and corn.

Cut avocados in half. Remove seeds. While still in skin, cut in thin slices in both directions. Spoon into soup. Mix. Simmer 1 minute.

Ladle into soup bowls. Garnish with chives. Serve warm.

AVOCADO & CARROT SOUP

2 cups CARROT JUICE

1 large AVOCADO

1 CORN cob, kerneled

¼ tsp VEGETABLE SEASONING

¾ cup chopped SUNFLOWER SPROUTS

Always peel carrots when making juice. Pour into 2-qt. saucepan and bring to a simmer.

Cut avocado in half. Remove seed. While still in skin, cut thin slices in both directions. Scoop out with soup spoon. Add to soup with corn. Simmer 1 minute.

Ladle into soup bowls. Garnish with sprouts. Mix sprouts lightly with a fork. Serve warm.

SERVES TWO

AVOCADO "BACON" & TOMATO SOUP

1/3 cup WATER

3 tbsp IMITATION BACON CHIPS

3 cups chopped TOMATOES, liquefied

¾ medium CUCUMBER, peeled, chopped

¼ cup CUCUMBER, peeled,
    diced small (set aside)

2 medium HAAS AVOCADOS

WATERCRESS

Bring water to a boil in small saucepan. Add bacon chips. Remove from heat.

Put tomatoes and larger cucumber in blender and liquefy. Remove avocado pulp from 1 and ½ of the avocados with a spoon, and add to blender. Blend until creamy. Pour into 2-qt. saucepan. Heat slowly.

Take the avocado half and cut thin slices in both directions while still in skin. Add to saucepan with diced cucumber.

Remove bacon chips with a slotted spoon. Add to saucepan. Don't discard water at this point. Heat slowly until soup starts to bubble.

The bacon chips are very strong flavored. Taste the soup. If you want a stronger flavor, add the water they reconstituted in.

Ladle into soup bowls, and garnish with watercress. Serve warm.

SERVES TWO

AVOCADO & CAULIFLOWER STEW

2 cups CAULIFLOWER florets

3 pats BUTTER

1 small ONION, chopped

2 tbsp BRAGG's LIQUID AMINOS

3 cups chopped TOMATOES, liquefied

2 PLUM TOMATOES, diced

1 medium ZUCCHINI, chopped

2 medium HAAS AVOCADOS, seeds removed

2 tbsp mild, fresh SALSA

Steam cauliflower 6 minutes.

Meantime in a 3-qt. saucepan sauté onion in butter 3 minutes.

Add aminos, tomatoes and zucchini to blender and liquefy.

Remove seeds from avocado. Spoon 1 and ½ of the avocados into blender. Blend.

Add liquid and salsa to stew. Simmer 2 minutes.

While other half of avocado is in skin, slice thin lines in both directions. Spoon into pot. Stir. Heat slowly until soup starts to bubble.

Ladle into soup bowls. Serve warm.

AVOCADO & PARSNIP SOUP

2 cups WATER

½ can CREAM OF CELERY SOUP

1 large PARSNIP, grated

2 medium AVOCADOS

3 tbsp PROGRESSO ROASTED PEPPERS

1 CHIVE, minced (optional)

Bring water to a boil. Add celery soup. Blend and simmer.

Cut avocados in half. Remove seeds. While still in skin, cut thin slices in both directions. Set aside.

Add parsnip to soup. Simmer 2 minutes.

Spoon avocado into soup. Add peppers. Simmer 1 minute.

Ladle into soup bowls. Garnish with chives. Serve warm.

SERVES TWO

CURRIED BROCCOLI & BARLEY SOUP*

½ cup uncooked PURLED BARLEY

1½ cups WATER

3 pats BUTTER

6 to 8 MUSHROOMS*, sliced

1 small ONION, chopped

1 cup WATER

2 cups small BROCCOLI, florets

¾ cup WATER

1 medium unpeeled
 ZUCCHINI, chopped

½ tsp VEGETABLE SEASONING

½ tsp CURRY POWDER

Soak barley overnight in 1½ cups water. Refrigerate. When preparing food drain well.

In a 3-qt. saucepan sauté barley and mushrooms in butter 3 minutes. Add onion and sauté 2 minutes longer.

Meantime steam broccoli 5 minutes. Save water for later use. Put ¾ cup of water into blender with zucchini. Liquefy.

Remove steamer from pot. Pour steaming water into 3-qt. saucepan.

Add zucchini and seasoning. Mix. Bring to a boil. Add broccoli. Simmer with cover on 2 minutes. Ladle into soup bowls. Serve warm.

*Never clean mushrooms under water. Wipe clean with a wet cloth.
*This dish requires overnight soaking of barley.

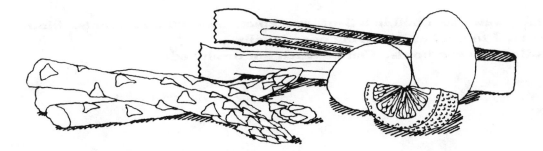

SERVES TWO

BROCCOLI STEM SOUP

4 BROCCOLI STEMS, peeled, halved, chopped small

1¼ cups WATER

1 medium ONION, halved, sliced

1 medium CARROT, peeled, grated

½ cup chopped WALNUTS

Steam broccoli stems 6 minutes.

Add onion to broccoli and steam 2 minutes longer.

Transfer broccoli stems and onion to blender with steaming water. Blend until creamy. Add more water if necessary. Add small amounts gradually for the consistency you want.

Return vegetables to pot. Add carrots. Heat. Simmer with cover on 2 minutes.

Ladle into soup bowls. Garnish with walnuts. Serve warm.

CONTINENTAL BORSCHT

2 cups WATER

1 small ONION, chopped

2 small BEETS, grated

1 medium CARROT, grated

1½ cups shredded CABBAGE

½ tsp VEGETABLE SEASONING

Bring water to a boil in a 3-qt. saucepan. Add all ingredients. Simmer with cover on 7 to 8 minutes stirring occasionally.

Ladle into soup bowls. Can be eaten hot or chilled.

SERVES TWO

CABBAGE SOUP

2 cups WATER

2 cups shredded CABBAGE

½ cup CELERY slivers
  diagonally

1 small POTATO, diced small

1 small ONION, chopped

½ tsp VEGETABLE SEASONING

2 PARSLEY sprigs, minced

1 dry BAY LEAF

3 tbsp IMITATION BACON
  CHIPS

2 medium CARROTS, peeled,
  sliced

½ cup PEAS (optional)

Bring water to a boil. Add all ingredients except carrots and peas. Simmer with cover on 4 minutes stirring occasionally.

Add carrots. Simmer 2 minutes. Add peas. Turn off heat. Keep on grill 1 minute with lid on.

Ladle into bowls. Serve immediately.

NOTE: Whether you use fresh or frozen peas, the instructions are the same. There's no need to cook fresh peas, and frozen peas are already blanched. Frozen peas merely need defrosting.

SERVES TWO

CAULIFLOWER SOUP

2 cups CAULIFLOWER florets

1¼ cups WATER

1 medium CARROT, peeled,
 coarsely grated

3 pats BUTTER

1 medium ONION, chopped

1 small CELERY rib, diced

¾ cup WATER

½ package of KNORR'S
 CAULIFLOWER SOUP

½ cup fresh PEAS or
 chopped STRING BEANS

Steam cauliflower 5 minutes using 1¼ cups water. If using string beans, add with cauliflower. Add carrots and steam 2 minutes longer.

Meantime in a 3-qt. saucepan sauté onion and celery in butter 3 minutes. Blend. Remove steamer from pot. Add ¾ cup water and cauliflower soup. Blend. Add to water used for steaming. Add steamed vegetables. Mix. If using peas, add now. Simmer with cover on 1 minute.

Ladle into soup bowls. Serve warm.

CREAM of CAULIFLOWER STEW

1 cup WATER

1 small head CAULIFLOWER, chopped

2 pats BUTTER or 1 tbsp OLIVE OIL

1 medium ONION, chopped

1 medium CARROT, coarsely grated

1 cup WATER

½ can CREAM OF CELERY SOUP

¼ tsp VEGETABLE SEASONING

1 CORN cob, kerneled

2 tbsp chopped PIMENTO

SERVES TWO

Steam cauliflower 4 minutes using 1 cup of water. Add carrot and steam 2 minutes longer. Save water for later use in soup.

Meantime use a small saucepan, sauté onion in butter 2 minutes.

Remove steamer from pot. Keep cauliflower covered with lid. Add 1 cup water and celery soup to steaming water. Blend. Heat.

Add onions, corn and seasoning. Turn off heat. Leave on hot grill 1 minute.

Ladle into soup bowls and garnish with pimento. Serve warm.

CREAMY CARROT & AVOCADO SOUP

1½ cups fresh CARROT JUICE

1 medium ZUCCHINI, chopped

  (need 1¼ cups)

½ cup chopped WALNUTS

1 large HAAS AVOCADO

¼ medium CUCUMBER, peeled

  diced

½ tsp VEGETABLE SEASONING

handful ALFALFA SPROUTS,

  cut in thirds

Make carrot juice. Remove seed from avocado. Cut thin sliced in both directions while still in skin. Set aside.

Pour carrot juice in blender. Add zucchini and walnuts. Liquefy. Spoon one half of the avocado in blender. Blend until smooth. Pour into pot. Add other half of avocado, the ¼ cucumber and sprouts. Heat slowly until soup bubbles.

Ladle into soup bowls. Serve warm.

SERVES TWO

BARLEY & CARROT JUICE SOUP*

½ cup uncooked PURLED BARLEY

1½ cups WATER

3 pats BUTTER

1 small ONION, chopped

1 small CELERY RIB, diced

½ cup WATER

1½ cups CARROT JUICE

1 medium-small ZUCCHINI, halved, thinly sliced

¾ cup chopped PARSLEY

½ cup chopped walnuts

Soak barley overnight in 1½ cups water. Refrigerate. When preparing meal drain well.

In a 3-qt. saucepan sauté barley in butter 3 minutes. Add onions and celery and sauté 3 minutes longer.

Add zucchini and parsley. Simmer with cover on 4 minutes.

Ladle into soup bowls, and garnish with walnuts. Serve warm.

*This dish requires overnight soaking of barley.

CARROT STEW*

½ cup uncooked PURLED BARLEY ½ can CREAM OF CELERY SOUP

2 cups WATER

3 pats BUTTER

1 small ONION, chopped

2 medium CARROTS, peeled, sliced

1 small bunch SPINACH, stems
 removed

¼ tsp VEGETABLE SEASONING
 (optional)

SERVES TWO

Soak barley overnight in 1½ cups water. Refrigerate. When preparing meal drain well.

Melt butter in a large skillet. Sauté barley 3 minutes. Add onion and sauté 3 minutes longer.

Meantime in a 3-qt. saucepan bring 2 cups of water to a boil. Add carrots and simmer with cover on 2 minutes.

Stir in celery soup. Heat. Add barley and onions. Mix.

Add spinach to pot. Simmer 1 minute.

This soup is so flavorful, you may want to taste it before seasoning.

Ladle into bowls. Serve warm.

*This dish requires overnight soaking of barley.

EGGPLANT & TOMATO STEW

3½ cups chopped TOMATOES

2 cups EGGPLANT, diced small,

1 small ONION, chopped small

1 large GARLIC clove, minced

2 fresh BASIL leaves, minced

1 tbsp fresh OREGANO leaves, minced

1 tbsp VIRGIN OLIVE OIL

½ GREEN BELL PEPPER, diced

PARMESAN CHEESE

Liquefy tomato in blender. Pour into 3-qt. saucepan. Add all ingredients except pepper. Bring to a slow boil. Simmer 8 minutes stirring occasionally.

Add pepper and simmer 2 minutes longer.

Ladle into soup bowls. Sprinkle with cheese. Serve warm.

SERVES TWO

CORN CHOWDER

2 cups WATER
1 cup RED or WHITE POTATO, peeled, diced
1 small ONION, chopped
1 small CELERY rib, chopped
½ can CREAM OF CELERY SOUP
2 pats BUTTER
2 CORN cobs, kerneled
2 sprigs PARSLEY, minced
½ tsp DEHYDRATED VEGETABLE SEASONING

Bring water to a boil. Add potato, onion, and celery. Return to a boil and simmer 3 minutes.
Add celery soup, butter and corn. Reserve ½ cup. Simmer 1 minute.
Ladle soup into blender and puree. Add ½ cup corn. Don't blend. Mix with wooden spoon.
Pour into soup bowls. Garnish with parsley. Serve warm.

CHEESY CORN CHOWDER

1½ cups WATER
1 medium POTATO, peeled, diced small
1 medium PARSNIP, grated
3 pats of BUTTER
1 small ONION, finely chopped
2 CORN COBS, kerneled or 2 cups
  frozen CORN

1 cup grated CHEDDAR CHEESE
1 cup chopped PARSLEY
½ tsp VEGETABLE SEASONING
1 CHIVE, minced (optional)

SERVES TWO

Cook potato in 1½ cups water 4 minutes. Add parsnip and steam 1 minute longer.

Meantime, sauté onion in butter 2 minutes in a small saucepan.

Liquefy potato and parsnip and <u>half</u> the corn in blender adding the steaming water slowly until you get the consistency desired. Add more hot water if necessary.

Transfer pureed mixture, and remaining kerneled corn to pot. Add seasoning and parsley. Bring to slow boil. Simmer 2 minutes.

Stir in cheese. Turn off heat. Leave on hot grill 1 minute.

Ladle into bowls. Garnish with chives. Serve warm.

EGG DROP SOUP

½ cup dried BLACK MUSHROOMS

2 cups WATER

2 tbsp dried ONION SOUP

1 tbsp DRY SHERRY (optional)

2 cups shredded SAVOY CABBAGE

2 SCALLIONS, minced

1 cup sliced CHINESE PEAS

½ cup BAMBOO SHOOTS

2 EGGS

2 pats BUTTER

2 sprigs PARSLEY, minced

Using 2 cups of water, soak mushrooms then squeeze dry. Save soaking water. Slice, discarding tough stems.

Add more water to soaking water to make 2 cups. In a 3-qt. saucepan, bring water to a boil. Add onion soup, sherry, cabbage, scallions and mushrooms. Return to a boil. Simmer 4 minutes.

Break egg yolk with a fork and stir slightly. Add Chinese peas, bamboo, eggs and butter. Simmer 2 minutes.

Ladle into soup bowls. Garnish with parsley. Serve warm.

SERVES TWO

ESCAROLE SOUP*

½ cup uncooked NAVY BEANS

4 cups WATER

½ cup sliced OKRAS

1 small RED BELL PEPPER,
  chopped

1 small ONION, chopped

3 tbsp IMITATION BACON CHIPS

1 small head ESCAROLE, chopped

3 pats BUTTER

½ tsp VEGETABLE SEASONING

Soak navy beans overnight in 1½ cups water. Refrigerate. When preparing meal drain well.

Bring 2½ cups water to a boil in a 3-qt. saucepan. Add beans. Simmer with cover on 4 minutes. Add okras, pepper, onion and bacon chips. Simmer 3 minutes longer.

Add escarole, butter and seasoning. Simmer 3 minutes.

Ladle into soup bowls. Serve warm.

*This dish requires overnight soaking of navy beans.

ZUCCHINI SOUP

1½ cups WATER

1 package ONION SOUP

1 large ZUCCHINI, chopped

1 medium-small ZUCCHINI,
  coarsely grated

1 large CARROT, coarsely grated

½ cup chopped PARSLEY

1 CORN cob, kerneled

4 PLUM TOMATOES, chopped

SERVES TWO

Bring water to a boil in a 3-qt. saucepan. Add onion soup. Simmer with cover on 2 minutes.

Meantime liquefy large zucchini in a blender. Add zucchini, carrot and chopped parsley. Cover and simmer 2 minutes.

Add plum tomatoes and corn. Simmer 1 minute.

Ladle into soup bowls. Serve warm.

ORIENTAL VEGETABLE SOUP*

½ cup uncooked PURLED BARLEY

3½ cups WATER

1 tsp VEGETABLE SEASONING

2 tbsp BRAGG'S LIQUID AMINOS

2 cups shredded SAVOY CABBAGE

1 tsp grated fresh GINGER ROOT

¼ cup DRY SHERRY

2 tbsp SAFFLOWER OIL

¼ cup chopped ONION

½ cup sliced MUSHROOMS

One 8 oz can sliced
 BAMBOO SHOOTS

¼ lb BEAN CURD (TOFU)
 cut into ½" chunks

1 cup SNOW PEAS, stems
 removed, string, cut
 bite-size

Soak barley in 1½ cups water overnight. Refrigerate. When preparing meal drain well. Bring 2 cups water to a boil in a 3-qt. saucepan. Add barley, seasoning, aminos, cabbage, ginger root and sherry. Simmer covered 6 minutes.

Meantime heat oil, and sauté onion and mushrooms in a small saucepan. Add all remaining ingredients to 3-qt. saucepan. Simmer 3 minutes. Ladle into soup bowls. Serve warm.

*This dish requires overnight soaking of barley.

SERVES TWO

BLACK BEAN SOUP*

½ cup uncooked BLACK BEANS

3½ cups WATER

¾ cup CELERY slivers

1 medium-small CARROT,
  coarsely grated

1 medium-small POTATO, peeled
  and diced

1 small ONION, chopped

½ can CREAM OF POTATO SOUP

1 tbsp minced, fresh OREGANO
  leaves

1 tsp minced, fresh SAVORY
  or BASIL leaf

Soak dry black beans in 1½ cups water overnight. Refrigerate. When preparing meal drain well.

Bring 2 cups water to a boil. Add black beans. Simmer with cover on 5 minutes stirring occasionally.

Add celery, carrot, potato and onion. Simmer 4 minutes. Add potato soup and herbs. Mix. Simmer 1 minute.

Ladle into soup bowls. Sprinkle with seasoning. Serve warm.

*This dish requires overnight soaking of beans.

CHICK PEAS & TOMATO SOUP*

1/3 cup uncooked CHICK PEAS (also known as garbanzo beans)

2 cups TOMATO JUICE from fresh tomatoes made in blender

½ cup diced CELERY

1 small bunch SPINACH, remove stems, chop

½ cup chopped NUTS (walnuts, almonds, or pecans)

WATERCRESS

SERVES TWO

Soak chick peas in 1½ cups distilled water overnight. When preparing meal drain well.

Combine chick peas and tomato in blender and liquefy. Pour into large pot. Add celery. Simmer covered 2 minutes.

Add spinach. Simmer 1 minute.

Ladle into soup bowls and sprinkle with nuts. Serve warm.

*This dish requires soaking chick peas overnight.

GREEN PEA SOUP*

½ cup uncooked SPLIT GREEN PEAS
3½ cups WATER
1 small ONION, chopped
1 medium HAAS AVOCADO, cut in
  half, remove seed

1 CARROT, grated finely
1 small ZUCCHINI, coarsely grated
½ tsp DILL SEED
2 sprigs PARSLEY, chopped

Soak split peas overnight in 1½ cups water. Refrigerate. When preparing meal drain well.

Bring 2 cups water to a boil. Simmer peas with cover on 7 minutes stirring occasionally. Add onion and simmer 2 minutes longer.

Transfer water, peas and onions to blender and blend until creamy. Scoop avocado out by the spoonful and add to blender. Blend.

Return to pot. Heat. Add carrot, zucchini and dill seed. Simmer 1 minute. Ladle into soup bowls. Garnish with parsley. Serve warm.

*This receipt requires overnight soaking of split peas.

SERVES TWO

LENTIL SOUP with KALE*

½ cup uncooked LENTILS

2 cups chopped TOMATOES, liquefied

1 dry BAY LEAF

1 small CELERY rib, diagonally sliced

2 medium-size CARROTS, sliced

¼ cup chopped PARSLEY

1 tbsp VIRGIN OLIVE OIL

½ cup diced ONION

1 large GARLIC clove, minced

1 small bunch KALE, chopped

3 PLUM TOMATOES, chopped

Soak lentils overnight in 1½ cups water. Refrigerate. When preparing meal drain well.

Pour tomatoes into a 3-qt. saucepan. Add lentils and bay leaf. Simmer covered 5 minutes stirring occasionally. Add celery, carrots and parsley and simmer 3 minutes longer.

Meantime heat oil in a small saucepan. Sauté onion 2 minutes. Add garlic and sauté 1 minute. Add to large saucepan. Add kale and simmer 2 minutes.

Ladle into soup bowls. Remove bay leaf. Garnish with plum tomatoes.

LENTILS, RUTABAGA & BRUSSELS SPROUTS SOUP*

½ cup uncooked LENTILS

3 cups WATER

½ can CREAM OF CELERY SOUP

¾ cup grated RUTABAGA

3 large BRUSSELS SPROUTS, sliced

2 tbsp SAFFLOWER OIL

1 small ONION, chopped

¾ cup CELERY RIB,
  slivered

½ tsp VEGETABLE SEASONING

1/3 cup chopped PARSLEY

SERVES TWO

Soak lentils overnight in 1 cup water. Refrigerate. When preparing meal drain well.

Bring 2 cups water to a boil in a 3-qt. saucepan. Add celery soup. Stir until blended. Add lentils, rutabaga and brussels sprouts. Simmer covered 7 minutes, stirring occasionally.

Meantime heat oil in a small saucepan and sauté onions and celery 2 minutes.

Add onions, celery and seasoning to soup. Cook 3 minutes longer.

Ladle into soup bowls. Garnish with parsley. Serve warm.

*This recipe requires overnight soaking of lentils.

VEGETABLE & LENTIL CHOWDER*

¾ cup uncooked LENTILS

3½ cups WATER

1 medium CARROT, grated

1 large TOMATO, liquefied

2 tbsp TOMATO PASTE

3 pats BUTTER

1 medium ONION, chopped

1 medium-small GREEN BELL PEPPER

1 tsp VEGETABLE SEASONING

1 dry BAY LEAF

3 PLUM TOMATOES, chopped small

GRATED PARMESAN CHEESE

Soak lentils overnight in 1½ cups water. Refrigerate. When preparing meal drain well.

Bring 2 cups water to a boil in a small saucepan. Add lentils. Simmer covered 7 minutes stirring occasionally.

Meantime in a 3-qt. saucepan sauté pepper in butter 2 minutes. Add onion and sauté 2 minutes longer.

Add lentils including the water plus carrot, tomato puree, tomato paste, seasoning and bay leaf to saucepan. Simmer 3 minutes. Remove bay leaf. Stir in plum tomatoes.

Ladle into soup bowls. Sprinkle with cheese. Serve warm.

*This recipe requires overnight soaking of lentils.

SERVES TWO

LIMA BEAN CHOWDER*

½ cup uncooked BABY LIMA BEANS

3½ cups WATER

3 tbsp CREAM OF CELERY SOUP

1 medium POTATO, peeled, diced small

1½ cups shredded CABBAGE

½ cup GREEN BELL PEPPER, diced

3 pats BUTTER

1 medium ONION, chopped

¼ tsp VEGETABLE SEASONING

½ cup shredded CHEDDAR
CHEESE

2 sprigs of PARSLEY, minced

Soak lima beans overnight in 1½ cups water. Refrigerate. When preparing meal drain well.

Bring 2 cups water to a boil in a 3-qt. saucepan. Add celery soup and lima beans Heat. Simmer covered 4 minutes, stirring occasionally. Add potato and cabbage and simmer 3 minutes longer. Add pepper and simmer another 3 minutes.

Meantime melt butter in a small saucepan. Sauté onion 2 minutes. Add to soup.

Stir in seasoning and cheese. Heat briefly.

Ladle into soup bowls. Garnish with parsley. Serve warm.

*This dish requires the pre-soaking of lima beans overnight.

SERVES TWO

ITALIAN MINESTRONE SOUP*

½ cup uncooked KIDNEY BEANS

3½ cups WATER

2 tbsp VIRGIN OLIVE OIL

1 medium ONION, chopped

½ cup diced CELERY RIB

2 small ZUCCHINI, cut ½" thick

2 GARLIC cloves, minced

2 tbsp TOMATO PASTE

1 large CARROT, peeled,
  thinly sliced

½ tsp VEGETABLE SEASONING

1 small bunch SPINACH, stems
  removed

2 tbsp grated PARMESAN CHEESE

Soak kidney beans overnight in 1½ cups water. When preparing meal drain well.

Bring 2 cups water to a boil in a 2-qt. saucepan. Add kidney beans and simmer covered 6 minutes stirring occasionally.

Meantime heat oil in a 3-qt. saucepan. Sauté onion, celery and zucchini 2 minutes. Add garlic and sauté 1 minute longer.

Add kidney beans and boiling water to saucepan. Stir in tomato paste, carrot, and seasoning. Simmer 3 minutes.

Add spinach. Simmer 1 minute.

Ladle into soup bowls. Sprinkle with cheese. Serve warm.

*This recipe requires soaking lima beans overnight.

SERVES TWO

CREAM of OKRA & MUSHROOM STEW

1 cup WATER

1 cup sliced OKRAS

1 medium CARROT, peeled, sliced

3 pats BUTTER

1 cup sliced small-size MUSHROOMS

¾ cup CELERY slivers

½ can MUSHROOM SOUP

1 CORN cob, kerneled

¼ tsp VEGETABLE SEASONING

Steam okra and carrot 5 minutes using 1 cup of water in steamer. Reserve water for stew.

Meantime in a 3-qt. saucepan, and sauté mushrooms and celery in butter 3 minutes.

Remove steamer. Keep lid over vegetables to keep warm. Pour steaming water into 3-qt. saucepan. Add mushroom soup. Heat and mix. Stir in remaining ingredients. Simmer covered 1 minute.

Ladle into soup bowls. Serve warm.

CHINESE PEAS, MUSHROOMS & PEPPER STEW

1 can CREAM OF MUSHROOM SOUP
½ soup can WATER
1 cup sliced MUSHROOMS, cut in half if large
1 cup sliced CHINESE PEAS
1 medium RED BELL PEPPER, diced
½ cup chopped PARSLEY

Combine mushroom soup and water in saucepan. Bring to a slow boil. Add remaining ingredients. Simmer 5 minutes.

SERVES TWO

SNOW PEAS, MUSHROOMS & OKRA STEW

1 can CREAM OF MUSHROOM SOUP

½ soup can WATER

¾ cup sliced OKRAS

1½ cups SNOW PEAS, halved

¾ cup sliced MUSHROOMS

½ cup fresh BABY ONIONS

½ cup chopped PARSLEY

Combine soup and water in a 3-qt. saucepan and bring to a slow boil. Add vegetables and simmer 5 minutes.

POTATO CHOWDER

3 pats BUTTER

1 small ONION, quartered, sliced

2 cups WATER

½ tsp VEGETABLE SEASONING

2 tbsp IMITATION BACON CHIPS

2 medium-size NEW WHITE or RED POTATOES, peeled, grated

1 medium-size CARROT, grated

½ can CREAM OF POTATO SOUP

1 bunch SPINACH, stems remove

In a 3-qt. saucepan melt butter. Sauté onion 2 minutes. Add water and bring to a boil. Add seasoning, bacon chips, potatoes and carrot and simmer covered 4 minutes.

Stir in potato soup. Heat. Add spinach and simmer 1 minute.

Ladle into soup bowls. Serve warm.

SERVES TWO

POTATO, ESCAROLE & STRING BEANS

2 cups WATER

1 package DRY ONION SOUP

2 medium NEW WHITE or RED
  POTATOES, julienned

1 handful STRING BEANS, tips removed
  slivered

2 SCALLIONS, chopped

1 small bunch ESCAROLE,
  halved, sliced

1 medium-large CARROT,
  peeled, sliced

Bring water to a boil. Add dry onion soup. Add all ingredients in order given.
Simmer 4 minutes.

Add escarole and carrots. Simmer 3 minutes longer.

Ladle into soup bowls. Serve warm.

POTATO SOUP

2 cups WATER

3 cups diced POTATOES

3 pats BUTTER

1 medium ONION, chopped

½ cup diced CELERY

2 tbsp BRAGG'S LIQUID AMINOS

1 medium-small ZUCCHINI,
  chopped

1 medium CARROT, peeled, grated

4 cups chopped KALE

½ tsp VEGETABLE SEASONING

1/3 cup chopped CHIVES

SERVES TWO

Bring 2 cups water to a boil in a 2-qt. saucepan. Add potatoes and simmer covered 5 minutes.

Meantime melt butter in a 3-qt. saucepan. Sauté onion and celery 3 minutes.

After potatoes are done, put aminos and zucchini in a blender and liquefy. Remove 2 cups of the cooked potatoes with a strainer spoon. Add to blender. Pour 1 cup of the boiling water into the blender. (Leave remaining water and potatoes in the pot.) Blend until smooth.

Combine all ingredients in 3-qt. saucepan. Simmer 3 minutes.

Ladle into soup bowls. Garnish with chives. Serve warm.

POTATO, SPINACH & OKRA STEW

2 cups WATER

2 medium-large NEW POTATOES, peeled, diced small

1 cup sliced OKRAS

½ can CREAM OF POTATO SOUP

¼ tsp DEHYDRATED VEGETABLE SEASONING

1 bunch SPINACH, stems removed

2 tbsp chopped PIMENTOS

Steam potatoes and okras 4 minutes using 1 cup of water. Reserve water for use in stew.

Remove steamer. Keep lid over vegetables. Add 1 cup of water, potato soup and seasoning to steaming water. Bring to a simmer. Return vegetables to pot. Add spinach and simmer covered 1 minute.

Ladle into soup bowls. Garnish with pimentos. Serve warm.

SERVES TWO

SWEET POTATO SOUP

2 cups WATER

2 cups coarsely grated SWEET POTATO

½ cup diced CELERY

½ tsp ALLSPICE

3 pats BUTTER

1/3 cup PARSLEY, chopped

Bring water to a boil. Add potato, parsnip and celery. Simmer covered 3 minutes.

Using a slotted serving spoon remove half of the vegetables. Set aside in a covered bowl.

Puree the remainder of the soup in an electric blender. Return puree to the pot and add the reserved vegetables, allspice, butter and parsley. Reheat.

Ladle into soup bowls. Serve warm.

TURNIP & BOK CHOY SOUP

2 cups WATER

1 package DRY ONION SOUP

1 medium TURNIP, grated

4 cups sliced BOK CHOY

3 pats BUTTER

¼ cup PROGRESSO ROASTED
   PEPPERS, chopped

Bring water to a boil. Add onion soup and turnip. Simmer covered 4 minutes. Add cabbage and simmer 3 minutes. Stir in butter and peppers and simmer 1 minute.

Ladle into soup bowls. Serve warm.

SERVES TWO

CREAMY PARSNIP & TOMATO STEW

3 cups chopped TOMATOES

1 cup chopped ZUCCHINI,

2 cups peeled and grated PARSNIPS

1 tbsp minced, fresh THYME LEAF

½ tsp VEGETABLE SEASONING

3 pats BUTTER

1 medium ONION, chopped

6 slices PLUM TOMATOES

Liquefy tomatoes and zucchini in a blender. Pour into 3-qt. saucepan. Add parsnip, herbs and seasoning. Bring to a slow boil. Simmer 5 minutes.

Meantime in a small saucepan, melt butter. Sauté onions 2 minutes.

Add onions to saucepan. Simmer 2 minutes longer.

Ladle soup into bowls. Garnish with tomato slices. Serve warm.

SNOW PEAS, MUSHROOMS & OKRA STEW

1 cup WATER

1¼ cups SNOW PEAS, cut bite-size

¾ cup sliced MUSHROOMS

½ cup sliced OKRAS

½ cup fresh BABY ONIONS

½ can CREAM OF MUSHROOM SOUP

¾ cup WATER

2 pats BUTTER

½ tsp VEGETABLE SEASONING

Steam vegetables 4 minutes using 1 cup water. Reserve for use in stew.

Remove steamer. Combine soup, water and butter and bring to a simmer.

Stir in vegetables and seasoning. Simmer covered 2 minutes.

Ladle into soup bowls. Season. Serve warm.

SERVES TWO

TOMATO & BARLEY SOUP*

½ cup uncooked PURLED BARLEY

1½ cups WATER

3 pats BUTTER

1 small ONION, chopped

3 large, ripe TOMATOES, quartered

3 stems BOK CHOY, halved, chopped

1 small ZUCCHINI, coarsely grated

2 PLUM TOMATOES, chopped

½ cup fresh PEAS

¼ cup PARSLEY, minced

Soak barley overnight in 1½ cups water. Refrigerate. When preparing meal drain well. In a 3-qt. saucepan melt butter. Sauté barley and onion 3 minutes.

Meantime liquefy the 3 large tomatoes in blender. Add to saucepan. Turn heat on medium. Add bok choy. Simmer covered 2 minutes. Add plum tomatoes and zucchini. Simmer 2 minutes. Stir in peas. Turn heat off. Leave on hot grate covered 1 minute.

Ladle into soup bowls. Garnish with parsley. Serve warm.

*This dish requires overnight soaking of barley.

SERVES TWO

CREAM of TOMATO SOUP

1 cup CAULIFLOWER florets

2 pats BUTTER

1 small ONION, chopped

2 cups TOMATO JUICE, made

from fresh tomatoes

1 medium ZUCCHINI, peeled, liquefied in

blender (swirl some of the tomato

juice in blender to flush out

remaining zucchini)

½ tsp VEGETABLE SEASONING

1 CORN cob, kerneled

6 slices PLUM TOMATOES

¼ cup chopped CHIVES

Steam cauliflower 5 minutes.

Meantime melt butter in a 3-qt. saucepan. Sauté onion 2 minutes.

Add juice to saucepan. Bring to a slow simmer. Add zucchini, seasoning and cauliflower. Simmer covered 2 minutes.

Add corn. Turn heat off. Leave on hot grate 1 minute.

Ladle into bowls. Garnish with tomato slices and chives. Serve warm.

SERVES TWO

Notes

SALAD ENTRÉES

ARTICHOKE HEARTS, BROCCOLI & ESCAROLE

2½ cups **BROCCOLI** florets

small head **ESCAROLE**, cut down spine,
  sliced 2" wide

1 medium-large **CUCUMBER**, peeled,
  chopped

1 **GARLIC** clove, minced

1 tbsp minced, fresh **BASIL**

1 tsp minced, fresh **OREGANO**

7 oz jar **ARTICHOKE HEARTS**
  packed in water

PARMESAN CHEESE

Steam broccoli 4 minutes. Add escarole and steam 2 minutes longer.

Put cucumber, garlic and herbs in blender. Liquefy. Warm up on small saucepan.

Remove escarole from steamer with tongs. Place on dinner dish. Place broccoli on top. Cut artichokes in half from stem to top. Place around broccoli.

Pour dressing over top. Sprinkle with cheese.

SERVES TWO

ARTICHOKE HEARTS & STRING BEAN SALAD*

¼ cup diced TOMATILLO

1 cup WATER

2 tbsp PICKLING SPICES

1 cup APPLE CIDER VINEGAR

¾ cup fresh BABY ONIONS

1/3 cup chopped fresh PARSLEY

2 cups slivered GREEN
  STRING BEANS

2 cups SUNFLOWER SPROUTS

7 oz jar ARTICHOKE HEARTS
  packed in water

Put first 6 ingredients in a 2-qt. saucepan. Heat.

Add string beans and simmer 8 minutes.

Spread sunflower sprouts on dinner dishes. Drain vinegar from pot. Remove any inedible spices. Spoon over sprouts.

Cut large artichokes in half from stem to top. Scatter on top.

ARTICHOKE HEARTS, POTATO* & SPINACH SALAD*

2 medium RUSSET POTATOES, *baked and refrigerated several hours

2 tbsp VIRGIN OLIVE OIL

½ cup diced CELERY

1 SCALLION, chopped small

1 GARLIC clove, minced

1 tbsp minced BASIL

2 tbsp BRAGG'S LIQUID AMINOS

1 medium ZUCCHINI, chopped

2 tbsp chopped PIMENTOS

1 small bunch SPINACH, stems removed

7 oz jar ARTICHOKE HEARTS packed in water

SERVES TWO

In a small saucepan heat oil. Sauté celery and scallion 2 minutes. Add garlic and basil and sauté 1 minute longer.

Put aminos and zucchini in blender. Liquefy. Add to saucepan. Heat slowly. Stir in pimentos. Simmer 2 minutes.

Prepare a bed of spinach on dinner dishes.

Cut potatoes (keep skins on) in half and slice. Spread over spinach.

Cut larger artichokes in half from stem to top. Spread over potatoes.

Spoon dressing over top.

ASPARAGUS & PARSNIP PLATTER

½ lb ASPARAGUS

1 medium-large PARSNIP, peeled, grated

1 medium CARROT, peeled, grated

1 small bunch SPINACH, stems removed

2 tbsp BRAGG'S LIQUID AMINOS

1 medium CUCUMBER, peeled, chopped

½ tsp VEGETABLE SEASONING

½ cup chopped WALNUTS

Snap off white ends of asparagus. Steam whole in a large pot 3 minutes. Add parsnip and carrots. Steam 2 minutes longer.

Meantime prepare a bed of spinach on dinner dishes.

Blend aminos, cucumber, seasoning and walnuts in blender.

Remove asparagus only with tongs and place together toward center of dish.

Sprinkle parsnips and carrots across the center of the asparagus to the edge of the plate.

Pour dressing over entire dish.

SERVES TWO

AVOCADO & EGG PLATTER with "BACON"

1/3 cup WATER

3 tbsp IMITATION BACON CHIPS

2 tbsp VIRGIN OLIVE OIL

1 RED BELL PEPPER, seeded, chopped

1 small ONION, quartered, sliced

4 tbsp BRAGG'S LIQUID AMINOS

1 small bunch SPINACH

½ tsp VEGETABLE SEASONING

2 large HAAS AVOCADOS,
  seeds removed

2 EGGS, hard boiled

Pour hot water over bacon chips. Set aside.

Heat oil in small skillet. Sauté pepper and onion 4 minutes. Remove from heat. Stir in 2 tbsp aminos. Keep covered.

Prepare a bed of spinach on dinner dishes. Sprinkle 2 tbsp aminos and seasoning over spinach.

Spoon avocados out of skin. Set in center of each dish. Slice egg in egg slicer in both directions. Sprinkle over entire dish.

Remove imitation bacon chips with a slotted spoon and sprinkle over eggs. Spoon pepper and onion over top.

AVOCADO SPINACH SALAD

2 tbsp VIRGIN OLIVE OIL

¾ cup sliced MUSHROOMS

3 fresh BASIL leaves, minced

2 tbsp fresh, mild SALSA

4 tbsp BRAGG's LIQUID AMINOS

1 small bunch SPINACH, stems
  removed

2 medium HAAS AVOCADOS, seed removed

4 PLUM TOMATOES, chopped

1 medium-small ZUCCHINI, grated

SERVES TWO

Heat oil in small pan. Sauté mushrooms and basil on medium-low heat 3 minutes. Stir in salsa and 2 tbsp aminos. Turn off heat. Keep on hot grate.

Prepare a bed of spinach on dinner dishes. Sprinkle 2 tbsp aminos over spinach. Spoon avocadoes out of skin. Slice each one in 6 sections. Place around dish in a spoke design.

Sprinkle tomatoes and zucchini over avocados.

Spoon mushrooms and dressing over top.

CAULIFLOWER, APPLE & BEET SALAD

2½ cups CAULIFLOWER florets

1 medium BEET, grated

1 cup WATER

½ LEMON

2 yellow-skin APPLES, cored, diced

1 cup APPLE JUICE

½ cup diced CELERY

1/3 cup chopped WALNUTS

¼ tsp ALLSPICE

ROMAINE LETTUCE, cut down spine, chopped

Put beets in a small bowl. Squeeze lemon into water and pour over beets. Set aside.

Put apples in a small bowl and cover with apple juice.

Steam cauliflower 5 minutes.

Drain beets well and add to steaming cauliflower. Steam 3 minutes.

Remove cauliflower and beets from steamer. Refrigerate 5 minutes.

Prepare a bed of lettuce on dinner dishes.

Put apple juice, celery, walnuts and spice in blender and liquefy.

Place cauliflower and beets over lettuce.

Sprinkle apples over vegetables. Pour apple dressing over top.

SERVES TWO

CAULIFLOWER, AVOCADO & CORN SALAD

2 cups CAULIFLOWER florets

1 CORN COB, kerneled

1 medium CUCUMBER, peeled, chopped

1 small TOMATILLO, chopped

1 tsp BRAGG'S LIQUID AMINOS

½ tsp VEGETABLE SEASONING

1 medium bunch SPINACH,
  stems removed

1 large HAAS AVOCADO

½ cup sliced BLACK OLIVES
  (optional)

Steam cauliflower 7 minutes. Remove to covered casserole to cool slowly. Meantime, kernel corn.

Put cucumber, tomatillo, aminos, and seasoning in blender. Get a firm hold on top and bottom and gently shake until contents liquefy.

Prepare a bed of spinach on dinner dishes.

Cut avocado in half. Remove pit. Keep avocado in skin while cutting thin slices in both directions. Remove with spoon when ready to use.

Layer cauliflower, avocado, and corn over spinach.

Pour cucumber dressing over top. Garnish with olives.

CAULIFLOWER, TOMATOES & SPINACH SALAD

2 cups CAULIFLOWER florets

1 small bunch SPINACH, stems removed

2 tbsp BRAGG'S LIQUID AMINOS chopped

1 small CUCUMBER, peeled, chopped

3 tbsp mild SALSA

½ cup MIXED BEAN SPROUTS

2 small HAAS AVOCADOS

2 medium TOMATOES,
  chopped

SERVES TWO

Steam cauliflower 7 minutes.

Make a bed of spinach on dinner dishes.

Cut avocados in half. Remove seeds. While still in skin, cut slices in both directions. Set aside.

Put aminos and cucumber in blender. Hold blender firmly while rocking back and forth until ingredients are creamy. Add salsa and stir with a long wooden spoon.

Put bean sprouts, avocados and tomatoes and cauliflower in a small bowl and combine. Scoop over spinach.

Pour dressing over top.

JICAMA SALAD

1 medium JICAMA, cut in small cubes

2 medium CARROTS, grated

½ cup diced CELERY

½ cup fresh PEAS

¼ tsp CUMIN SEED

2 tbsp BRAGG'S LIQUID AMINOS

1 medium CUCUMBER, peeled, chopped

1 small TOMATILLO, chopped

½ tsp DEHYDRATED
     VEGETABLE SEASONING

1 small bunch SPINACH, stems
     removed

1/3 cup sliced BLACK OLIVES

Combine jicama, carrots, celery, peas and cumin seed in a bowl.

Put aminos, cucumber, tomatillo and seasoning in blender and liquefy. Pour over vegetables and mix well.

Make a bed of spinach. Scoop mixture on top.

Garnish with olives.

SERVES TWO

POTATO SALAD*

5 to 7 small RED POTATOES,
  *baked and refrigerated 2 hours
  or more
1 cup total diced RED and
  YELLOW BELL PEPPER

1/3 cup diced CELERY
3 tbsp grated DAIKON
2 sprigs PARSLEY, minced
1 small TOMATILLO, minced

DRESSING

1 tbsp BRAGG'S LIQUID AMINOS
1 medium-large CUCUMBER, peeled, chopped
1 medium-small TOMATILLO, chopped
¼ tsp DILL SEED
¼ tsp powdered KELP

Scrub potatoes well. Put in pot. Cover with water. Bring to a boil. Simmer covered until barely done (about 5 to 8 minutes depending on size).

Discard water. Fill pot with cold water. Drain several times until potatoes are cooled. Put potatoes in a covered casserole dish and refrigerate overnight.

When ready to prepare meal dice potatoes and combine with vegetables. Refrigerate.

Put aminos, cucumber and tomatillo in blender. Blend until creamy. Add seasoning. Swirl. Pour over vegetables and mix. Serve warm, or if you prefer, chill for 15 minutes.

SERVES TWO

POTATO & VEGETABLE PLATTER*

1 small bunch SPINACH, stems removed

1 cup SNOW PEAS, stems removed

2 medium RUSSET POTATOES, *baked and refrigerated 2 hours or more

2 medium CARROTS, grated

½ cup CELERY slivers

2 tbsp BRAGG'S LIQUID AMINOS

1 medium CUCUMBER, peeled, chopped

1 small TOMATILLO, chopped

¼ tsp DILL SEED

1/3 cup sliced BLACK OLIVES (optional)

Prepare a bed of spinach on dinner dishes. Place snow peas over top in a spoked wheel design. Scatter potatoes, carrots and celery over top.

Put aminos, cucumber and tomatillo in blender and liquefy. Pour over vegetables. Sprinkle with dill seed.

Garnish with olives.

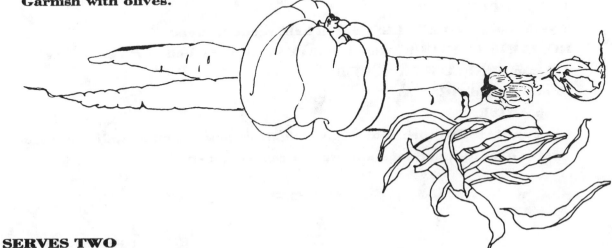

SERVES TWO

ZUCCHINI & GREEN BEANS

2 cups slivered GREEN BEANS

2 medium ZUCCHINI, sliced

1 small YELLOW ⸱ QUASH, julienned

2 tbsp BRAGG'S LIQUID AMINOS

1 small TOMATILLO, chopped

1 small CUCUMBER

½ tsp VEGETABLE SEASONING

2 cups ALFALFA SPROUTS

1/3 cups sliced BLACK OLIVES

First, steam green beans 4 minutes. When done, transfer to a covered casserole for cooling.

Prepare the other foods while the beans are cooling.

Put aminos, tomatillo, cucumber and seasoning in a blender and liquefy.

Sprinkle sprouts on dinner dishes. Combine first three vegetables and scatter on sprouts. Pour dressing on top. Garnish with olives.

YAM & APPLE SALAD

2 cups coarsely grated YAMS

1 cup APPLE JUICE

2 yellow-skinned APPLES, cut in half, seeded, sliced

ROMAINE LETTUCE, sliced thin. Enough for a bed of greens for two.

1/3 cup SUNFLOWER SEEDS

½ cup grated JICAMA

1 tsp ANISE

1/3 cup RAISINS (pre-soaked overnight, or pour ½ cups boiling drinking
  water over top, and let stand while preparing dish).

SERVES TWO

Pour apple juice over apples in a small bowl.

Steam yams 2 minutes. Remove from heat.

Meantime prepare a bed of romaine lettuce on dinner dishes.

Pour from ½ to ¾ cup apple juice from bowl and put in blender with sunflower seeds. Blend until smooth. Combine yams, apples, jicama, anise, and raisins. Scatter over lettuce. Pour apple dressing over top.

THREE-BEAN SALAD*

1/3 cup DRY GARBANZO BEANS

½ cup DRY KIDNEY BEANS

handful STRING BEANS, one
   variety or combination

2 cups DRINKING WATER

1 cup APPLE CIDER VINEGAR

1 large TOMATILLO, chopped

2 tbsp finely grated fresh GINGER

1 tbsp PICKLING SEASONINGS

1 tbsp fresh, minced
   BASIL LEAVES

1 medium TOMATILLO, diced

½ medium CUCUMBER, grated
   (can leave skin on if
   organic)

2 cups SUNFLOWER SPROUTS

Put large tomatillo, ginger, seasoning, oregano and water and vinegar in a 3-pt. saucepan. Heat.

Remove stem and string from string beans. Cut diagonally in bite-size pieces. Put garbanzos, kidney beans and string beans in saucepan. Mix. Simmer 10 minutes. Prepare a bed of sunflower sprouts.

Use a wide-hole serving spoon and spread beans on sprouts. Remove any large pieces of ginger and herbs. Not all the kidney beans will swell. Remove all small, bright red kidney beans before serving. Mix small tomatillo and cucumber together. Spoon over beans.

*NOTE: This recipe requires soaking beans overnight.

SERVES TWO

ZUCCHINI & AVOCADOS with CARROTS

2 tbsp BRAGG'S LIQUID AMINOS

1 tbsp VIRGIN OLIVE OIL

1 tbsp LEMON JUICE

1 large GARLIC clove, minced

1 tsp minced BASIL

1 medium ZUCCHINI, julienned

1 large CARROT, grated

1 SCALLION, chopped

2 cups ALFALFA SPROUTS

1 large HAAS AVOCADO

¼ cup sliced BLACK OLIVES

Put aminos, oil, juice, garlic and basil in a blender or nut chopper. Swirl until blended.

Combine zucchini, carrot, scallion and sprouts.

Cut avocado in half. Remove pit. Cut thin slices in both directions while still in skin. Remove meat with a tablespoon and mix with other vegetables.

Pour dressing over top. Garnish with olives.

SERVES TWO

VEGETABLE ENTREÉS

ASPARAGUS, PARSNIP & CARROT

¾ lb ASPARAGUS, cut bite-size

1 large PARSNIP, peeled, grated

1 medium CARROT, peeled, grated

3 pats BUTTER or 2 tbsp
ALMOND OIL

Use a large skillet and heat butter on medium heat. Sauté asparagus 4 minutes. Keep cover on. Mix occasionally.

Add parsnip and carrot. Sauté 2 more minutes. Turn with spatula several times.

This dish is so tasty there is no need to season it!

ASPARAGUS, PARSNIP & OKRA

¾ lb ASPARAGUS cut bite-size

½ cup diced RED BELL PEPPER

4 large OKRAS, sliced

1 medium-large PARSNIP, peeled,
grated

4 heaping tbsp ALMOND
BUTTER

3 tbsp WATER

1 CORN cob, kerneled

Steam asparagus, pepper and okra 3 minutes. Add parsnip. Steam 2 minutes longer. If you are using frozen corn, add 1 cup now.

Meantime, put almond butter in blender or nut chopper with enough water to make a thin syrup.

Place vegetables on dinner plate. Pour almond syrup over top. Sprinkle with corn.

SERVES TWO

ASPARAGUS & RUTABAGA

1 small RUTABAGA, grated

¾ lb ASPARAGUS, cut bite-size

3 stems BOK CHOY, cut down
  center, thin slivers

½ cup diced RED BELL PEPPER

3 pats BUTTER

2 tbsp BRAGG'S LIQUID AMINOS

2 tbsp WATER

½ tsp ALLSPICE

1/3 cup SILVERED ALMONDS

Steam rutabaga 3 minutes.
Add asparagus, bok choy, and pepper and steam 5 minutes longer.
Remove steamer with vegetables from pot. Cover vegetables to keep warm.
Discard steaming water. Put butter, aminos, water and allspice in pot. Heat.
Return vegetables to pot. Mix.
Spoon onto dinner dishes. Sprinkle with almonds.

BEETS, CAULIFLOWER & OKRAS

4 small BEETS, julienned

2½ cups CAULIFLOWER florets

¾ cup sliced OKRAS

3 pats BUTTER

2 tbsp BRAGG'S LIQUID AMINOS

½ tsp CARAWAY SEEDS

¼ cup sliced BLACK OLIVES (optional)

Layer beets then cauliflower in steamer basket. Steam 4 minutes. Add okras
and steam 3 minutes longer.
Remove steamer. Cover vegetables to keep warm.
Discard steaming water. Combine butter, aminos and caraway seeds in pot.
Bring to a simmer. Add vegetables. Mix well.
Garnish with olives.

SERVES TWO

BEETS & SAVOY CABBAGE

2 medium BEETS, julienned

3 cups sliced SAVOY CABBAGE

1 medium ONION, quartered, sliced

½ tsp DILL

3 pats BUTTER

2 tbsp BRAGG'S LIQUID AMINOS

Steam beets 3 minutes. Add cabbage and onion and steam 4 minutes longer.

Remove steamer from pot. Cover vegetables. Drain water. Heat butter and aminos. Add dill and vegetables. Mix.

Serve warm.

BROCCOLI, CORN & RED PEPPER

3 cups BROCCOLI florets

1 tbsp VIRGIN OLIVE OIL

3 pats BUTTER

1 large RED BELL PEPPER,
  halved, seeded, sliced

¾ cup sliced MUSHROOMS

1 large GARLIC clove, minced

1 CORN, kerneled

½ tsp VEGETABLE SEASONING

Steam broccoli 5 minutes.

Meantime heat oil and butter in large skillet. Sauté pepper and mushrooms 4 minutes. Add garlic and sauté 1 minute longer. Add corn and sauté 1 minute.

Put broccoli on dinner dishes. Scoop mixture over top. Season.

SERVES TWO

BROCCOLI, SAVOY CABBAGE & CARROTS

2½ cups BROCCOLI florets

3 cups sliced SAVOY CABBAGE

1 large CARROT, slivered

¼ cup grated DAIKON or chopped ONION

1/3 cup WATER

3 pats BUTTER

½ can CREAM OF
  MUSHROOM SOUP

¼ cup chopped WALNUTS
  (optional)

Steam broccoli and cabbage 4 minutes. Add carrot and daikon. Steam 2 minutes longer.

Meantime combine water, butter and soup in a small saucepan. Heat.

Place vegetables on dinner dish. Pour sauce over top.

Sprinkle with walnuts.

BROCCOLI SOUFFLÉ

3 cups chopped BROCCOLI

¾ cup sliced OKRAS

1 small ONION, chopped

1/3 cup WATER

½ can CREAM OF BROCCOLI SOUP

3 pats BUTTER

1 ear CORN, kerneled

3 tbsp chopped PIMENTOS

1 cup grated CHEDDAR
  CHEESE

Steam broccoli, okra, and onion 4 minutes.

Preheat broiler.

Remove steamer. Cover vegetables to keep warm. Combine water, soup and butter and bring to a simmer. Add remaining ingredients, reserving ¼ cup cheddar cheese.

Pour into greased baking pan. Sprinkle remaining cheese on top. Broil on lowest rack until cheese starts to bubble about 2 minutes.

SERVES TWO

BROCCOLI, TOMATOES & ZUCCHINI

2½ cups BROCCOLI florets

2 BOK CHOY STEMS, cut down center, sliced, keep tops separate. Chop.

½ cup sliced MUSHROOMS

1 med. ZUCCHINI, unpeeled, grated

1½ cups diced TOMATO

2 tbsp BRAGG'S LIQUID AMINOS

½ tsp VEGETABLE SEASONING

1/3 cup chopped WALNUTS

Steam broccoli, bok choy <u>stems</u>, and mushrooms 4 minutes. Add bok choy <u>tops</u> and steam 1½ minutes longer.

Remove steamer from pot. Discard water. Combine all vegetables and seasoning and mix.

Garnish with walnuts.

BRUSSELS SPROUTS, RUTABAGA & CARROTS

1 medium RUTABAGA, peeled, grated

4 medium BRUSSELS SPROUTS, thinly sliced

1 large CARROT, peeled, grated

1/3 cup WATER

½ can CREAM OF CELERY SOUP

3 pats BUTTER

1 tbsp fresh minced

   BASIL

Steam rutabaga 3 minutes. Add brussels sprouts and steam 3 minutes. Add carrot and steam 1 minute longer.

Remove steamer. Cover vegetables to keep warm.

Combine water, soup, butter and basil. Heat.

Spoon vegetables on dinner dishes. Pour dressing over top.

SERVES TWO

BRUSSELS SPROUTS SOUFFLÉ

2½ cups BRUSSELS SPROUTS, halved lengthwise

¾ cup sliced MUSHROOMS

½ cup WATER

½ cup CREAM OF MUSHROOM SOUP

2 pats BUTTER

1 medium ZUCCHINI, grated

½ cup chopped PARSLEY

½ cup sliced BLACK OLIVES

1 cup grated CHEDDAR CHEESE

Steam brussels sprouts 3 minutes. Reserve water for later. Add mushrooms and steam 3 minutes longer.

Preheat broiler.

Remove steamer from pot. Cover vegetables to keep warm. Combine water, soup, butter, zucchini and parsley. Heat.

Add vegetables, olives and ¾ cup cheese. Mix.

Pour into greased baking dish. Sprinkle remaining cheese on top. Broil until cheese starts to bubble, about 2 minutes.

CABBAGE, APPLE & WALNUTS

6 cups sliced CABBAGE

3 pats BUTTER

2 tbsp SAFFLOWER OIL

1 large ONION, halved, sliced

1 large APPLE, cored and sliced ½" thick

½ tsp ANISE SEED

½ tsp ALLSPICE

1/3 cup chopped WALNUTS

SERVES TWO

Steam cabbage 3 minutes.

Meantime, heat butter and oil in a large skillet. Sauté onion 2 minutes.

Transfer cabbage into skillet. Sauté 3 minutes. Sprinkle with anise. Spread apple slices on top. Sprinkle with allspice. Don't mix.

Simmer on medium-low heat 2 minutes.

Remove with spatula on to dinner dishes. Sprinkle with walnuts.

SAVOY CABBAGE, CHINESE PEAS & CARROTS

3 cups bowlful, thinly sliced
 SAVOY CABBAGE

1 cup sliced CHINESE PEAS

1 large CARROT, grated

1 tbsp VIRGIN OLIVE OIL

1 GARLIC clove, minced

2 fresh BASIL leaves, minced

1/3 cup WATER

½ can CREAM OF CELERY
 SOUP

Steam cabbage 3 minutes. Add peas and carrot and steam 2 minutes longer.

Meantime heat oil in a small skillet. Sauté garlic and basil 1 minute. Add water and soup. Stir while heating.

Scoop vegetables on dinner dishes. Pour sauce over top.

SERVES TWO

CABBAGE & THREE-PEPPER CASSEROLE

6 cups shredded CABBAGE

1 each, small RED, YELLOW and
GREEN BELL PEPPERS, pulp and
seed removed, sliced in rings

2 tbsp SAFFLOWER OIL

2 pats BUTTER

1 medium ONION, halved,
sliced

1 tsp CARAWAY SEED

Steam cabbage and peppers 4 minutes.
Meantime heat oil and butter in a large skillet. Sauté onion 1 minute.
Transfer cabbage and peppers to skillet. Sauté 3 minutes.
Sprinkle with caraway seed.

RED CABBAGE & CORN

6 cups shredded RED CABBAGE

½ cup sliced OKRAS

1 CORN cob, kerneled (don't scrape
cob yet)

2 tbsp BRAGG'S LIQUID AMINOS

1 medium-large ZUCCHINI, chopped

3 pats BUTTER

1 tsp VEGETABLE SEASONING

¼ cup sliced BLACK OLIVES

Steam cabbage and okras 4 minutes. Add corn and steam 1 minute longer.
Put aminos, cream from corn cob, and zucchini in blender. Liquefy.
Remove steamer from pot. Keep lid over vegetables to keep warm. Discard
water. Put butter in pot and add zucchini. Heat.
Add vegetables and seasoning. Mix.
Garnish with olives.

SERVES TWO

SAVOY CABBAGE, AVOCADO & PEAS

4 cups shredded SAVOY CABBAGE

1 cup fresh PEAS

2 medium HAAS AVOCADOS

2 tbsp BRAGG'S LIQUID AMINOS

1 med-large ZUCCHINI, chopped

½ tsp VEGETABLE SEASONING

3 pats BUTTER

3 tbsp PIMENTOS (optional)

Steam cabbage 5 minutes. Add peas and steam ½ minute longer.

Meantime, cut avocados in half. Remove seed. While still in skin, cut in both directions. Set aside.

Put aminos, zucchini, the pulp of 1 avocado, and seasoning in blender. Blend until creamy. Remove steamer from pot. Cover vegetables to keep warm. Discard water. Melt butter in pot. Add zucchini/avocado sauce. Heat.

Place cabbage and peas on dinner dishes. Scatter second avocado over vegetables. Pour dressing over top.

Garnish with pimentos.

CABBAGE, RED PEPPER & CHINESE PEAS

1 tbsp VIRGIN OLIVE OIL

3 pats BUTTER

3 cups sliced CABBAGE

¾ cup sliced OKRAS

1 RED BELL PEPPER, tops, seeds and
  pulp removed

2 SCALLIONS, sliced

¼ cup PINE NUTS (optional)

Heat oil and butter in large skillet on medium-low. Add vegetables in order given.

Lower heat and sauté 3 minutes. Mix and sauté 2 minutes longer.

SERVES TWO

SWEET & SOUR RED CABBAGE

3 cups shredded RED CABBAGE	3 pats BUTTER
½ cup sliced OKRA	2 tbsp HONEY
½ cup sliced MUSHROOMS	1 tbsp MOLASSES
1 small ONION, halved, sliced	2 tbsp fresh LEMON JUICE
2 tbsp SAFFLOWER OIL	2 tbsp SWEET PICKLE RELISH

Soak cabbage in water 10 minutes.

Heat oil and butter in large skillet. Add okra, mushrooms and onion and sauté 2 minutes with cover on.

Drain cabbage well. Add to skillet. Cover and simmer 3 minutes on medium-low.

Meantime in a small saucepan, mix together honey, molasses, lemon juice and sweet pickles. Pour evenly over vegetables in skillet. Simmer on lowest heat 3 minutes.

RED CABBAGE & PARSNIPS with ALMOND SAUCE

6 cups shredded RED CABBAGE	3 heaping tbsp ALMOND
1 medium-large PARSNIP, peeled, grated	BUTTER
½ cup fresh PEAS	¼ tsp ALLSPICE
¼ cut WATER	¼ cup ALMOND
	SLIVERS (optional)

Steam cabbage 3 minutes. Add parsnips and steam 2 minutes longer. Add peas and steam ½ minute.

Put water and almond butter in a nut chopper or food processor and blend.

Spoon vegetables on dinner dishes. Sprinkle with allspice. Pour nut sauce over top. Garnish with almonds.

SERVES TWO

ESCAROLE, TURNIPS & CORN

1 tbsp VIRGIN OLIVE OIL

1 small ONION, quartered, sliced

1 GARLIC clove, minced

½ can CREAM OF ONION SOUP

1/3 cup WATER

1 cup grated TURNIP

1 small bunch ESCAROLE, halved, sliced

1 CORN cob, kerneled

1 small jar ROASTED PEPPERS

Heat oil in 3-qt. pot. Sauté onion 2 minutes. Add garlic and sauté 1 minute longer.

Add soup with water. Heat. Add turnip and simmer covered on medium-low 4 minutes.

Add escarole. Simmer 1 minute. Add corn and peppers. Simmer 1 minute longer.

CARROTS, KALE & MUSHROOMS

4 medium CARROTS, thinly sliced

1 medium ONION, halved, sliced

1 cup sliced MUSHROOMS

1 small bunch KALE, chopped

2 tbsp BRAGG'S LIQUID AMINOS

1 medium-large ZUCCHINI, chopped

3 pats BUTTER

½ tsp VEGETABLE SEASONING

Steam carrots, onion and mushrooms 4 minutes.
Add kale and steam 1 minute longer.
Meantime put aminos and zucchini in blender and liquefy.
Remove steamer from pot. Discard water. Add zucchini and butter. Heat.
Blend in vegetables and seasoning.

SERVES TWO

CARROT & SPINACH CRUNCH

2 large CARROTS, slivered

1 medium PARSNIP, sliced thin

1 bunch SPINACH, stems removed

2 tbsp WATER

1 small ZUCCHINI, chopped

3 pats BUTTER

½ tsp VEGETABLE SEASONING

½ cup chopped ALMONDS

2 tbsp slivered ALMONDS

Steam carrots and parsnip 3 minutes. Add spinach and steam 1 minute longer.

Put water and zucchini in a blender or nut chopper. Liquefy. Pour into small saucepan with butter. Heat. Add seasoning.

Transfer vegetables to a bowl with chopped almonds. Mix. Scoop onto dinner dishes. Pour sauce over top. Sprinkle with almonds.

VEGE BURGERS

1 cup finely grated CARROT

½ cup diced GREEN BELL PEPPER

¾ cup grated ZUCCHINI

1 small CORN cob, kerneled

1 EGG

¼ cup diced CELERY

¼ cup minced ONION

4 sprigs PARSLEY, minced

½ cup ground SUNFLOWER
 SEEDS

1/3 cup BREAD CRUMBS

3 tbsp SAFFLOWER OIL

Steam carrots and pepper 2 minutes. Add zucchini. Steam 1 minute longer.

Scramble egg in a large bowl. Add corn, celery, onion and parsley. Mix. Add steamed vegetables. Mix. Add sunflower seed meal. Mix. Gradually add bread crumbs for consistency needed to make patties.

Heat oil on high heat in large skillet or use grill. Fry patties 1 minute on each side. Lower heat to medium-high and fry 1 minute longer on each side. Keep covered each time.

Serve with sliced tomato and sunflower sprouts.

SERVES TWO

CAULIFLOWER, PEAS & EGGS

3 cups CAULIFLOWER florets

1 cup chopped PARSLEY

2 EGGS, lightly scrambled

2 tbsp OLIVE OIL

2 pats BUTTER

½ cup fresh PEAS

½ tsp VEGETABLE SEASONING

Steam cauliflower 4 minutes. Remove from steamer. Add parsley and steam 1 minute.

Heat oil and butter in a large skillet. Fry cauliflower 2 minutes on medium-high.

Pour in eggs. Add peas and parsley. Fry until eggs are cooked, turning with a spatula. Season.

SERVES TWO

CAULIFLOWER, SNOW PEAS & CORN

3 cups CAULIFLOWER florets

1 cup SNOW PEAS, cut in half

1 CORN cob, kerneled

ITALIAN PESTO

1/3 cup PINE NUTS* (also called pignolia nuts)

1 small GARLIC clove, minced

1/3 cup OLIVE OIL

½ cup minced, tightly packed fresh BASIL LEAVES

1 tbsp fresh, minced OREGANO LEAVES

2 sprigs PARSLEY, minced

Grind nuts and garlic in blender.
Slowly add oil. Add herbs and blend.
Stop several times to scrape down sides of blender.
Steam cauliflower 5 minutes. Add snow peas and steam 2 minutes longer.
Remove steamer from pot. Discard water. Use pot to combine all three vegetables.
Scoop on to dinner dishes.
Spoon Italian Presto Dressing over top.

*NOTE: Pine nuts are expensive. Walnuts can be used in place of pine nuts. Trader Joe's Specialty Stores in California have the most reasonably priced pine nuts.

SERVES TWO

CAULIFLOWER, AVOCADO & KALE

3 tbsp **IMITATION BACON CHIPS**

1 medium **CARROT**, grated

3 cups **CAULIFLOWER** florets

1 small bunch **KALE**, stems removed, chopped

2 tbsp **BRAGG'S LIQUID AMINOS**

1 medium-small **ZUCCHINI**, chopped

3 pats **BUTTER**

1 large **AVOCADO**

Pour 1/3 cup hot water over bacon chips. Set aside.

Steam cauliflower in a large steamer 5 minutes. Add carrot. Steam 1 minute. Add kale and steam 1 minute longer.

Meantime liquefy aminos and zucchini in blender.

Transfer vegetables to bowl. Keep covered with pot lid to keep warm. Pour zucchini in pot. Add butter and strained bacon chips. Heat.

Remove seed from avocado. While still in skin, cut thin slices in both directions. Set aside.

Combine carrot, cauliflower and kale in bowl. Spoon onto dinner dishes. Remove avocado with a spoon and scatter over vegetables.

Pour sauce over top.

VARIATION: Replace kale with corn.

SERVES TWO

CAULIFLOWER, KALE & CARROT

3 cups CAULIFLOWER florets

1 SCALLION, minced

1 large CARROT, grated

1 small bunch KALE, torn from stem,
  chopped

1/3 cup WATER

3 pats BUTTER

½ can CREAM OF CAULIFLOWER
  SOUP

½ cup sliced BLACK OLIVES
  (optional)

Steam cauliflower 4 minutes in a large steaming pot.

Add scallion and carrot and steam 2 minutes longer. Add kale and steam 1 minute longer.

Transfer vegetables to a covered bowl.

Combine water, butter and soup. Heat.

Spoon vegetables onto dinner dishes. Pour sauce over top. Garnish with olives.

EGGPLANT PATTIES

2 tbsp IMITATION BACON CHIPS

1 lb EGGPLANTS, halved, sliced ½" thick

½ cup diced ONION

1 cup finely grated CARROT

1 EGG

½ cup chopped PARSLEY

½ cup BREAD CRUMBS

3 tbsp OLIVE OIL

Pour 1/3 cup hot water over bacon chips. Set aside.

Steam eggplant 6 minutes. Add onion and carrot and steam 2 minutes longer.

Scramble egg in large bowl. Add parsley and steamed vegetables. Smash eggplant with a fork until it blends with egg. Add strained bacon chips. Mix in bread crumbs until "Pastey." Add more bread crumbs gradually if necessary.

Heat oil on medium-high in a large skillet. Using a large serving spoon drop mixture into skillet. Brown patties 2 minutes on each side.

Serve with tomatoes, and sunflower sprouts.

SERVES TWO

EGGPLANT, SPINACH & TOMATOES

3½ cups **JAPANESE EGGPLANTS,**
  chopped small

2 **SCALLIONS,** chopped

3 tbsp **OLIVE OIL**

2 large **TOMATOES,** quartered

4 **PLUM TOMATOES,** chopped

1 tbsp minced, fresh **BASIL**

1 tsp minced, fresh **OREGANO**

1 bunch **SPINACH,** stems removed

PARMESAN CHEESE

¼ cup sliced **BLACK OLIVES**

Steam eggplant 5 minutes.

After eggplant is steamed, heat oil in a large skillet over medium-high. Sauté eggplant and scallions 3 minutes.

Put large tomatoes in blender and liquefy.

After eggplant is brown, add both tomatoes and seasonings to skillet. Simmer 3 minutes.

Meantime reheat steaming water and steam spinach 1 minute.

Serve with spinach on the side or mix with eggplant. Sprinkle with cheese. Garnish with olives.

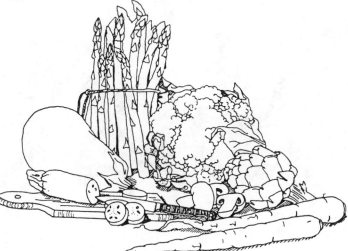

SERVES TWO

EGGPLANT CREOLE

3½ cups JAPANESE EGGPLANTS
  chopped small

1 small GREEN BELL PEPPER, diced

2 tbsp OLIVE OIL

1 medium ONION, chopped

1 GARLIC clove, minced

2 large TOMATOES, pureed

3 PLUM TOMATOES, diced

3 tbsp mild SALSA

1 CORN cob, kerneled

1/3 cup sliced OLIVES

    If using a regular eggplant, cut from top to bottom twice like a pinwheel. The purpose of this is to have skin on each piece.

    Steam eggplant 5 minutes. Add pepper and steam 2 minutes longer.

    When eggplant is done, heat oil in a large skillet and sauté eggplant, onion and garlic 3 minutes.

    Add pureed tomato, plum tomatoes and salsa. Simmer 4 minutes. Add corn and simmer 1 minute.

    Garnish with olives.

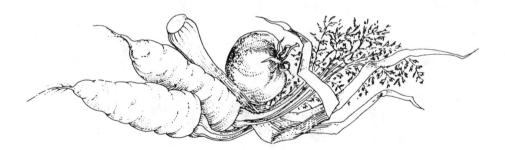

SERVES TWO

CREAMED CORN PIE*

Pie Shell (prepare first)

½ cup raw SUNFLOWER SEEDS
½ cup raw ALMONDS
3 tbsp ALMOND OIL

*Soak sunflower seeds and almonds separately overnight in 1 cup of water.

When ready to prepare meal, drain seeds and kernels separately in a wire strainer with a shaking motion to extract more water. Dry off further by tossing in a dish towel.

Grind seeds and almonds in a food processor. If you don't have one, use a nut chopper, but put a small amount in at a time, removing contents each time. When using a nut chopper, grind seeds and kernels separately - they take different times to grind.

Transfer to small bowl and add oil. Mix well. Scoop into a pie dish or two shallow soup bowls. Spread with a sliding motion using a tablespoon. Refrigerate.

FILLING

3 tbsp BUTTER
1 tbsp SAFFLOWER OIL
2 large CORN cobs, kerneled
1 medium PARSNIP, grated

½ cup fresh SWEET PEAS
1 EGG, scrambled
¼ tsp ALLSPICE

Be sure to scrape corn cob with a paring knife to get all the cream off the cob. Combine all ingredients in a bowl. Heat butter and oil on medium-high in a large skillet.

Pour vegetables into skillet. Cover. Mix occasionally until egg is cooked. Return to bowl. Cool 3 minutes. Scoop mixture into pie shell.

SERVES TWO

76

GREEN BEANS, CARROTS & ZUCCHINI

2 cups slivered GREEN BEANS
2 SCALLIONS, chopped
1 cup grated CARROTS
1 medium ZUCCHINI, grated
1/3 cup WATER

3 pats BUTTER
½ can CREAM OF
  CELERY SOUP
¼ cup chopped WALNUTS

Steam beans and scallion 5 minutes. Add carrots and steam 2 minutes longer. Add zucchini and steam 1 minute.
Remove steamer from pot.
Heat water, soup and butter. Add vegetables. Mix.
Garnish with walnuts.

GREEN BEANS, PARSNIP & OKRA CRUNCH

2 cups slivered GREEN BEANS
¾ cup sliced OKRAS
1 medium PARSNIP, grated

2 heaping tbsp ALMOND BUTTER
1/8 to ¼ cup WATER
½ cup slivered ALMONDS

Steam beans and okra 4 minutes. Add parsnips and steam 2 minutes longer.
Meantime put almond butter in blender or nut chopper. Add 1/8 cup water. Blend. Add more water if necessary for a syrupy consistency.
Remove steamer. Discard water. Put vegetables in pot to combine.
Place vegetables on plate. Pour nut butter syrup on top.
Garnish with slivered almonds.

SERVES TWO

GREEN BEANS, CORN, MUSHROOMS & RED PEPPER

2 cups slivered GREEN BEANS

1 cup sliced MUSHROOMS

½ cup diced RED BELL PEPPER

1/3 cup WATER

½ can CREAM OF MUSHROOM SOUP

3 pats BUTTER

1 tbsp minced, fresh BASIL

1 CORN cob, kerneled

Steam beans, mushrooms and pepper 5 minutes.
Remove steamer from pot. Cover vegetables to keep warm.
Heat water, soup and butter. Add basil. Add all vegetables and mix.

STRING BEANS & RUTABAGA with CORN SAUCE

1 medium RUTABAGA, peeled and
  coarsely grated

2 cups slivered STRING BEANS

1 large CORN cob, kerneled (don't
  scrape cream off cob yet)

3 pats BUTTER

½ can CREAM OF CELERY SOUP

¼ cup WATER

¼ tsp ALLSPICE

Steam rutabaga 2 minutes. Add string beans and steam 4 minutes longer. Add half of the corn and steam 1 minute.

Meantime add other half of corn and the cream that was scraped off the cob, butter, soup, water and seasoning in a blender. Blend. Pour into small saucepan and heat.

Remove steamer from pot. Discard water. Return vegetables to pot and mix. Scoop on to dinner dishes. Pour sauce over top.

SERVES TWO

PARSNIP PANCAKES

1¾ cups finely grated PARSNIPS

1/3 cup minced ONION

¾ cup diced RED BELL PEPPER

1 EGG

½ cup BREAD CRUMBS

3 tbsp VIRGIN OLIVE OIL

1 bunch KALE

3 pats BUTTER

Steam parsnips, onion, and pepper 2 minutes. Transfer to a bowl. Add egg. Mix. Add bread crumbs. Mix. Add more bread crumbs if necessary to form into patties.

Heat oil in large skillet or on a grill. Fry on medium-high heat 2 minutes on each side.

Serve with steamed, buttered kale.

PARSNIPS & OKRA with TOMATOES

2 medium PARSNIPS, peeled, grated

¾ cup sliced OKRAS

1 bunch SPINACH

4 PLUM TOMATOES, diced

½ cup chopped WALNUTS

3 tbsp WATER

In a large steaming pot steam okra 2 minutes. Add parsnip and steam 1 minute longer. Add spinach and steam 1 minute. Add tomatoes and move away from heat. Keep covered.

Put chopped walnuts in a blender or nut chopper. Grind into a meal. Add water. Add more water if necessary to make a syrupy consistency.

Put vegetables on dinner dishes and mix. Pour walnut sauce over top.

SERVES TWO

PARSNIPS, CARROTS & OKRAS
with MUSHROOM SAUCE

¾ cup sliced OKRAS

½ cup sliced MUSHROOMS

2 cups PARSNIPS, peeled, grated

1 large CARROT, grated

3 sprigs PARSLEY, minced

3 pats BUTTER

1/3 cup WATER

½ can CREAM OF MUSHROOM
  SOUP

Steam okras and mushrooms 3 minutes. Add parsnips, carrot and parsley and steam 2 minutes longer.

Remove steamer from pot. Cover vegetables to keep warm. Heat water and butter. Add soup. Blend.

Scoop vegetables on dinner dishes and mix. Pour sauce over top.

PARSNIPS, PEAS & PEPPERS

2 cups sliced PARSNIPS

1 RED BELL PEPPER, seeded, halved, sliced

1 cup fresh PEAS or CHINESE PEAS

3 heaping tbsp ALMOND
  BUTTER

1/8 to 1/4 cup WATER

Steam pepper 2 minutes. Add parsnips and steam 1½ minutes longer. If using Chinese peas or frozen peas, add now. Add fresh peas after parsnips are done. Remove from heat. Keep covered.

Put almond butter and 1/8 cup water in nut chopper. Swirl. Add more water gradually if necessary to make a syrupy consistency.

Remove steamer from pot. Discard water. Put vegetables in pot to mix.

Scoop onto dinner dishes. Pour almond sauce over top.

SERVES TWO

PARSNIP PIE*

Pie Shell (prepare first)

½ cup raw SUNFLOWER SEEDS

½ cup raw ALMONDS

1/3 cup pre-soaked RAISINS

1/3 cup shredded COCONUT

3 tbsp ALMOND OIL

Follow directions for pie shell under Creamed Corn Pie recipe, except include raisins and coconut in the grinding process.

FILLING

2 cups grated PARSNIPS

1 medium-large CARROT, grated

1 small bunch SPINACH, stems removed,

1 CORN cob, kerneled (don't scrape cream

  of cob at this point)

3 pats BUTTER

¼ cup chopped ALMONDS

2 tbsp SLIVERED ALMONDS

Steam parsnips and carrots 2 minutes. Add spinach and corn and steam 1 minute longer.

Remove steamer from pot. Discard water. Move away from hot grate. Add butter and vegetables. Scrape the cream off the cob with a paring knife into the pot. Mix until butter is distributed. Add chopped almonds. Mix.

Scoop into pie shell and sprinkle with almonds.

*This dish requires overnight soaking of ingredients for pie shell. Also, this recipe takes about 30 minutes preparation time.

SERVES TWO

STUFFED PEPPER with YAMS & CORN

1¾ cups grated YAMS

1 tender rib of CELERY, diced

2 GREEN BELL PEPPERS, cut from bottom to top (so they lie sideways), remove pulp and seeds

1 CORN cob, kerneled

½ cup chopped PARSLEY

¼ tsp ALLSPICE

¾ cup chopped WALNUTS

1/3 cup WATER

Layer yams, celery and pepper. Steam 2 minutes.

Combine corn and parsley in a bowl and set aside. Be sure to scrape cream off cob.

Use tongs and remove peppers temporarily.

Add yams and celery to the bowl with corn and parsley. Mix. Return peppers to steaming pot for 1 minute.

Meantime put nuts in a nut chopper and grind into meal. Add water and swirl. Add more water in very small amounts if it's necessary to make a syrupy consistency.

Add to allspice to allspice and 2 tbsp of nut dressing to moisten.

Scoop into peppers. Pour remaining of dressing over top.

SERVES TWO

PLANTAIN & SAVOY CABBAGE

2 tbsp VIRGIN OLIVE OIL

3 cups sliced SAVOY CABBAGE

1 small GREEN BELL PEPPER, diced

1 large ripe PLANTAIN, peeled, sliced

3 large GREEN ONION, chopped

3 tbsp BRAGG's LIQUID AMINOS

Heat oil over medium-high heat in a wok or large skillet. Add cabbage and peppers. Stir-fry 1 minute. Add plantain and onion. Stir-fry 1 minute longer. Add aminos, lower heat to low. Simmer 3 minutes.

STUFFED PEPPER with EGGPLANT

1 lb JAPANESE EGGPLANTS, halved
  lengthwise, sliced ½" thick

2 BELL PEPPERS, slice from
  bottom to top. Remove pulp and seeds.

2 tbsp VIRGIN OLIVE OIL

1 large GARLIC clove, minced

3 medium TOMATOES, chopped

3 PLUM TOMATOES, diced

1 CORN cob, kerneled

¼ cup SUNFLOWER SEEDS

Steam eggplant 7 minutes. When done, replace lost water and steam peppers 3 minutes.

Heat oil in a large skillet. Sauté eggplant 3 minutes. Add garlic and sauté 1 minute longer.

Put medium tomatoes in a blender and liquefy. Pour into skillet. Heat. Add plum tomatoes and corn. Simmer 2 minutes.

Scoop mixture into peppers. Pour tomato sauce over top. Garnish with sunflower seeds.

SERVES TWO

POTATOES AU GRATIN

4 pats BUTTER

3 cups coarsely grated NEW POTATOES

1 medium ONION, chopped

1 bunch SPINACH

1 cup grated CHEDDAR CHEESE

PAPRIKA

Put butter in a medium-size bowl and keep near hot grate.
Preheat broiler.
Steam potatoes and onion 3 minutes. Add spinach and steam 1 minute longer.
Transfer to bowl. Add ¾ cup of cheese. Mix.
Scoop into greased baking dish. Sprinkle remaining cheese on top. Broil on bottom rack until cheese starts to bubble. About 2 minutes.
Sprinkle with paprika.

BAKED POTATO*, BROCCOLI & OKRA

2 RUSSET POTATOES*, baked and
  refrigerated the day before

2 cups BROCCOLI florets

¾ cup sliced OKRA

3 pats BUTTER

2 tbsp WHOLE WHEAT FLOUR

¾ cup MILK

¾ cup shredded CHEDDAR
  CHEESE

¼ tsp WORCESTERSHIRE
  SAUCE

Leave skin on potatoes and cut in half. Slice ½" thick. Steam with broccoli and okra 5 minutes.
Meantime in a small saucepan, over low heat, melt butter. Use a flat-edged-wooden spoon and stir in flour. Simmer 1 minute. Raise heat slightly. Gradually stir in milk stirring continuously. Add cheese. Simmer until cheese melts.

SERVES TWO

BAKED POTATO*, ESCAROLE & PEPPER

2 baked **RUSSET POTATOES**, *baked and
  refrigerated the day before
1 tbsp **VIRGIN OLIVE OIL**
3 pats **BUTTER**
1 **RED BELL PEPPER**, seeds and pulp
  removed, halved, sliced

1 package **ONION SOUP MIX**
½ cup **WATER**
10 to 12 **ESCAROLE** leaves,
  halved, sliced 2" thick

    Leave skins on potatoes and cut in half. Slice ½" thick.
    Heat oil and butter in skillet. Sauté potatoes 2 minutes turning occasionally.
Add pepper and sauté 2 minutes longer.
    Meantime dissolve soup in ½ cup of water. Add to skillet. Heat.
    Add escarole and cook 2 minutes.

BAKED POTATO*, RED CABBAGE & PEAS

2 baked **RUSSET POTATOES***, baked and
  refrigerated the day before
3 cups grated **RED CABBAGE**
¾ cup fresh **PEAS**
2 tbsp **SAFFLOWER OIL**

2 tbsp **BRAGG'S LIQUID
  AMINOS**
2 tbsp **KETCHUP**
1 tbsp **LIME or LEMON**
  juice

    Leave skin on potato and cut in half. Slice ½" thick. Steam potatoes and
cabbage 4 minutes.
    Meantime using a small saucepan, heat oil, aminos, ketchup and juice. Simmer
on low. Add peas 1 minute before the potatoes and cabbage are to be done.
    Scoop potatoes and cabbage on dinner dishes. Pour sauce over top.

SERVES TWO

BAKED POTATO*, SPINACH & MUSHROOMS

3 tbsp IMITATION BACON CHIPS

2 RUSSET POTATOES, *baked and
  refrigerated the day before

¾ cup sliced MUSHROOMS

1 bunch SPINACH, stems removed

2 tbsp BRAGG'S LIQUID AMINOS

1 small ZUCCHINI, chopped

3 pats BUTTER

Pour 1/3 cup of water over bacon chips. Set aside.

In a large pot, steam potatoes and mushrooms 4 minutes. Add spinach and steam 1 minute longer.

Meantime put aminos and zucchini in blender and liquefy. Scrape into small saucepan. Put 2 tablespoons water in blender and swirl to get rest of zucchini out. Pour into saucepan. Add butter. Simmer. Add strained bacon chips.

Scoop steamed vegetables on dinner dishes. Pour sauce over top.

RED POTATOES, WAX BEANS & KALE

4 to 5 small RED POTATOES

1½ cup slivered WAX BEANS

1 small bunch KALE, stems removed,
  chopped

½ cup chopped SCALLION

1/3 cup WATER

3 pats BUTTER

½ can CREAM OF POTATO SOUP

Scrub potatoes. Don't peel. Cover with water and boil until firm, about 5 to 6 minutes.

Meantime steam beans 4 minutes. Add kale and scallion, and steam 1 minute longer.

Remove steamer from pot. Cover vegetables to keep warm. Add water, butter and soup and heat.

Dice potatoes. Combine with remaining vegetables. Scoop onto dinner dishes. Pour sauce over top.

SERVES TWO

POTATO PANCAKES

1½ cups grated raw RUSSET POTATOES
1 EGG
¾ cup peeled, finely grated
  BROCCOLI STEMS

1 small ONION, diced
3 tbsp WHOLE WHEAT FLOUR
¼ tsp DILL SEED
2 tbsp SAFFLOWER OIL

Grate potatoes into bowl of water. Squeeze potatoes between hands until dry. (This removes excess liquid and surface starch).

Combine all ingredients except oil. Heat oil in large frying pan or on grill. Drop the potato mixture by ladlefuls into the hot oil and fry until browned. Turn to brown on second side.

Can be served with slices of tomato and avocado, or apple sauce, or cottage cheese, or yogurt, or cranberry sauce, or steamed spinach.

POTATO, ESCAROLE & CARROTS

¾ cup WATER
4 tbsp DRY ONION SOUP (usually 1 pkg)
2 medium-large NEW WHITE or RED
  POTATOES, julienned
1 medium-large CARROT, peeled, sliced

1 handful STRING BEANS, tips
  removed, slivered
1 SCALLION, sliced
6 cups sliced ESCAROLE or SAVOY
  CABBAGE

Bring water to a boil in a large pot. Add dry onion soup. Mix. Add all ingredients in order given. Cover. Simmer on low 5 minutes.

VARIATION: Can use rutabaga or turnip in place of potato.

SERVES TWO

POTATO, SPINACH & OKRA

2 cups julienned NEW WHITE or
  RED POTATOES
½ cup sliced OKRAS
1 bunch SPINACH, stems removed,
1 tbsp VIRGIN OLIVE OIL
2 pats BUTTER

2 pats BUTTER
1 GARLIC clove, minced
1 tbsp minced, fresh BASIL leaf
2 tbsp BRAGG's LIQUID AMINOS
One 3½ oz jar ROASTED PEPPER
  chopped

Steam potatoes and okras 5 minutes in a large steamer. Add spinach and steam 1 minute longer.

Meantime heat oil and butter in small saucepan. Sauté garlic 1 minute. Add basil, aminos and peppers (include water). Simmer 1 minute.

Pour sauce over top. Put vegetables on dinner dishes.

POTATOES, BROCCOLI & NUTS

2 medium NEW POTATOES, peeled,
  julienned
2 cups small BROCCOLI florets
½ can CREAM OF POTATO SOUP

1/3 cup DRINKING WATER
½ cup diced CELERY
½ cup chopped WALNUTS

Steam potatoes 2 minutes. Add broccoli and steam 4 minutes longer.

Meantime combine soup, water and celery in a small saucepan. Simmer 2 minutes.

Place potatoes and broccoli on dinner dishes. Pour sauce over top. Sprinkle with walnuts.

SERVES TWO

POTATO & CARROT HASH BROWNS

2 medium-size NEW WHITE or RED
 POTATOES, peeled, finely grated
2 medium-size CARROTS, peeled,
 finely grated
3" long piece of DAIKON, peeled,
 finely grated, or small ONION minced

1 EGG
½ cup BREAD CRUMBS
½ cup chopped PARSLEY
3 tbsp VIRGIN OLIVE OIL

Combine first four ingredients. Add bread crumbs and parsley. Mix. Form into patties.

Heat oil in large skillet or on grill. Over medium-high heat fry 2 minutes on each side. Lower heat. Fry 1 minute on each side.

Serve with steamed kale or spinach, or celery sticks.

POTATOES, SPINACH & "BACON"

4 tbsp BACON FLAVORED CHIPS
3 cups diced NEW POTATOES
1 small ONION, chopped
1 bunch SPINACH, stems removed

1/3 cup WATER
½ can CREAM OF POTATO SOUP
¼ tsp DILL SEED

Soak bacon chips in 1/3 cup hot water. Set aside.

Steam potatoes. Add onions and steam 2 minutes longer. Add spinach and steam 1 minute.

Remove steamer from pot. Cover vegetables to keep warm. Add water, potato soup and dill. Heat. Stir in vegetables and drained bacon chips and mix.

SERVES TWO

RUTABAGA, ASPARAGUS & CORN with
ALMOND BUTTER SAUCE

1 medium-large RUTABAGA, grated

¾ lb ASPARAGUS, white
  ends removed

1 CORN cob, kerneled, (don't scrape
  cream from cob yet)

1 medium-small ZUCCHINI
  peeled, chopped

3 heaping tbsp ALMOND BUTTER

Steam rutabaga 2 minutes. Add asparagus and steam 4 minutes longer.

Meantime put cream from corn, 1 tbsp of water and zucchini in blender.
Liquefy. Get a firm grip on the blender and shake until the solids have liquified.
Add almond butter. Blend. Add more water if necessary to make a creamy
consistency.

Remove asparagus with tongs and place in center across dinner dishes. Mix
rutabaga and corn together and spoon across asparagus.

Pour almond sauce over top.

SPINACH, TOMATO & CHEESE

1 tbsp VIRGIN OLIVE OIL

2 pats BUTTER

1 cup sliced MUSHROOMS

1 GARLIC clove, minced

1½ cups chopped TOMATOES

3 tbsp fresh, mild SALSA (optional)

1 bunch SPINACH, stems removed

1 cup grated natural CHEDDAR
  CHEESE

Heat oil and butter on medium-low in a large pot. Sauté mushrooms and garlic
2 minutes. Keep lid on throughout cooking process. Add tomatoes and salsa.
Simmer 1 minute. Add spinach and simmer 2 minutes longer.

Remove from heat. Sprinkle with cheese.

SERVES TWO

SPINACH, BRUSSELS SPROUTS & CORN

6 to 8 BRUSSELS SPROUTS, thinly sliced
  separate layers

1 large CARROT, peeled, grated

1 bunch SPINACH

1 CORN cob, kerneled

½ cup chopped TOMATOES

½ cup chopped WALNUTS

Steam brussels sprouts in a large steamer 3 minutes. Add carrot and steam 2 minutes longer. Add spinach and corn and steam 1 minute.

Meantime put walnuts in a nut chopper and grind to a meal. Put tomatoes in blender and liquefy. Add walnuts to blender and blend.

Spoon vegetables on dinner dishes. Pour sauce over top.

QUICHE LORRAINE*
Pie Shell (prepare first)

½ cup raw SUNFLOWER SEEDS

½ cup raw ALMONDS

3 tbsp ALMOND OIL

*Soak sunflower seeds and almonds separately overnight in 1 cup each of distilled water.

Follow directions for pie shell under Creamed Corn Pie.

FILLING

3 tbsp IMITATION BACON CHIPS

½ cup diced ONION

½ cup sliced OKRAS

1 cup sliced MUSHROOMS (use small
  ones)

1 bunch SPINACH, stems removed

1 CORN cob, kerneled

dash PAPRIKA (optional)

SERVES TWO

Pour 1/3 cup hot water over bacon chips and set aside.

If using frozen corn, cover 1 cup of corn with boiling water now. Set aside. (The dish will not be as flavorful though.)

Steam onion, okras and mushrooms 5 minutes using a large enough steamer to hold spinach.

Meantime kernel corn into a large bowl. Be sure to scrape the cob with a paring knife to get the cream off.

When 5 minutes are up for vegetables, add spinach and steam 1 minute longer.

Use tongs to remove spinach and place on a dinner dish. Cut into smaller pieces. Add remaining ingredients from steamer into bowl. Add strained bacon chips. Mix. Gradually add spinach to bowl and mix with other ingredients.

Scoop into pie shell. Sprinkle with paprika.

CHARD & CHEESE PIE
Pie Shell (Prepare first)
See Creamed Corn Pie Recipe

FILLING

1 cup sliced OKRAS

1 medium ZUCCHINI, grated

1 lb GREEN SWISS CHARD, stems removed, chopped

1 large, ripe TOMATO, chopped

1 cup grated CHEDDAR CHEESE

½ tsp DEHYDRATED VEGETABLE SEASONING

Steam okras 3 minutes. Add zucchini and chard and steam 1½ minutes longer. Remove steamer from pot. Combine all ingredients and mix very well. Scoop into pie shell or soup bowls.

SERVES TWO

CHARD PITA SANDWICH

2 tbsp VIRGIN OLIVE OIL

½ cup sliced MUSHROOMS

1 small ONION, thinly sliced

1 small RED or YELLOW BELL
 PEPPER, halved, thinly sliced

1 GARLIC clove, minced

1 lb CHARD, stems removed, chopped

3 tbsp PARMESAN CHEESE

½ tsp VEGETABLE SEASONING

2 PITA BREADS

Heat oil in large skillet. Sauté mushrooms, onion, and pepper 3 minutes. Add garlic. Sauté 1 minute longer.

Add chard and simmer 2 minutes. Remove chard with tongs, and put in strainer. Drain by pressing with a serving spoon. Spread out on platter to cool off.

Cut pita bread in half. Open pockets and stuff chard in first. Use a slotted spoon and put it in remaining ingredients.

Serve with celery sticks and cucumber slices.

KALE, PARSNIP & CARROT

1 medium-large PARSNIP, grated

1 medium-large CARROT, grated

1 small ONION, chopped

1 bunch KALE, stems removed, chopped

2 tbsp BRAGG'S LIQUID AMINOS

1 medium ZUCCHINI, unpeeled,
 chopped

3 pats BUTTER

1 tsp VEGETABLE SEASONING

Steam parsnip, carrot and onion 2 minutes. Add kale and steam 1 minute longer.

Meantime liquefy aminos and zucchini in blender.

Remove steamer from pot. Discard water. Cover vegetables to keep warm.

Melt butter in pot. Add zucchini. Heat. Add vegetables and seasoning. Mix.

SERVES TWO

STUFFED CHARD LEAVES

2 tbsp VIRGIN OLIVE OIL

1 small ONION, chopped

½ cup diced tender center of CELERY

1 medium ZUCCHINI, grated coarsely

1½ cups TOMATO JUICE, made from
  fresh tomatoes

3 tbsp mild SALSA

4 PLUM TOMATOES, diced

½ cup chopped PARSLEY

2 tbsp fresh, minced BASIL LEAVES

1 CORN cob, kerneled

4 large SWISS CHARD leaves

½ cup chopped OLIVES

Heat oil in a large skillet and sauté onion, celery and zucchini 2 minutes. Add tomato juice, salsa, plum tomatoes, parsley, and basil. Simmer 5 minutes stirring occasionally. Add corn and simmer ½ minute longer.

Meantime steam chard 2 minutes. When done, carefully transfer on a large platter.

Score raised side of stem on chard so it will roll. Keep raised side on bottom. Use a slotted spoon and drain mixture well from sauce and fill chard. Roll from stem end.

Place on dinner dishes. Add olives to sauce and mix. Pour sauce over top.

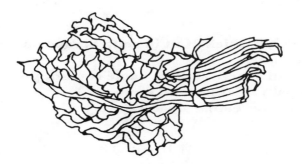

SERVES TWO

BUTTERNUT SQUASH, SAVOY CABBAGE & APPLES

2 cups grated BUTTERNUT SQUASH

3 cups sliced SAVOY CABBAGE

1 yellow, sweet APPLE, cored, cut
  in half, sliced

1/3 cup ALMONDS

2 or 3 tbsp WATER

1 tbsp MAPLE SYRUP (optional)

3 pats BUTTER

Slice squash 2" thick. Remove skin. Remove seeds. Grate.

Steam squash and cabbage 4 minutes. Add apples and steam 2 minutes longer.
Meantime put almonds in a nut chopper and grind to a meal. Add water slowly and
swirl until creamy.

Put almond liquid, maple syrup and butter in a small saucepan. Bring to a
simmer.

Place vegetables on dinner dishes. Pour sauce over top.

BUTTERNUT SQUASH, SNOW PEAS & CELERY

1 small BUTTERNUT SQUASH

1 cup SNOW PEAS, stems removed, string

1 cup CELERY slivered

1 cup chopped PARSLEY

1 tbsp SAFFLOWER OIL

3 pats BUTTER

½ tsp DEHYDRATED
  VEGETABLE SEASONING

Wash squash. Slice 3/8" thick. Cut in half. Scrape out pulp and seeds. Leave
unpeeled. Steam 5 minutes.

Heat oil and butter in a large skillet. Sauté squash, peas, celery and parsley 5
minutes. Stir occasionally. Season and serve.

Cut away skin as you are eating squash.

SERVES TWO

BUTTERNUT SQUASH PATTIES

2½ cups grated BUTTERNUT SQUASH

1/3 cup finely chopped ONION

¼ cup finely diced CELERY

1 EGG

1/3 cup minced PARSLEY

¼ cup ALMONDS, coarsely ground

1/3 cup SUNFLOWER SEEDS,
  coarsely ground

¼ cup BREAD CRUMBS

3 tbsp VIRGIN OLIVE OIL

Slice squash 2" thick. Remove skin. Cut in half. Scrape out seeds and pulp. Grate. Steam with onion and celery 3 minutes.

Scramble egg in a large bowl. Stir in parsley and steamed vegetables. Add almonds and sunflower seeds. Add bread crumbs if needed to form a patty. Mix well and form into patties.

Heat oil on medium-high in a large skillet. Fry patties 2 minutes on each side. Keep covered. Lower heat. Fry 1 minute on each side.

Serve with sunflower sprouts and celery sticks.

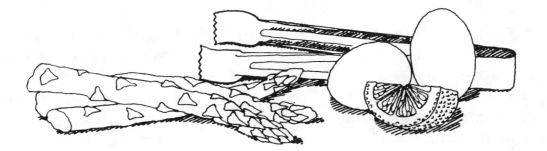

SERVES TWO

SQUASH ITALIANO

2 tbsp VIRGIN OLIVE OIL

1 small ONION, chopped small

1 large GARLIC clove, minced

2 large TOMATOES, pureed

3 or 4 PLUM TOMATOES, chopped small

3 tbsp mild SALSA

1 cup CAULIFLOWER florets,
  cut into small sections

½ cup each diced YELLOW and
  GREEN BELL PEPPERS

2 medium-small ZUCCHINI,
  sliced

1/3 cup sliced OLIVES

3 tbsp grated PARMESAN
  CHEESE

Heat oil in a large skillet. Sauté onions 1 minute. Add garlic and sauté 1 minute longer. Add all ingredients except cheese and olives. Simmer 6 minutes stirring occasionally.

Add olives. Mix.

Sprinkle with cheese when served.

SPAGHETTI SQUASH, SNOW PEAS & TOMATOES

½ of a medium size SPAGHETTI SQUASH

2 tbsp VIRGIN OLIVE OIL

2 SCALLIONS, chopped

1 GARLIC clove, minced

2 large TOMATOES, pureed

3 tbsp mild SALSA

1 cup chopped PARSLEY

4 PLUM TOMATOES, chopped
  small

1 cup SNOW PEAS, stems and
  strings removed, cut

STUFFED OLIVES

SERVES TWO

Slice squash 2" thick. Remove skins. Cut in half. Scrape out seeds and pulp. Grate coarsely.

Heat oil in a large skillet. Sauté scallions 1 minute. Add garlic and sauté 1 minute longer. Add pureed tomatoes, salsa, parsley and plum tomatoes. Heat. Add squash and simmer on low 5 minutes stirring occasionally.

Meantime steam snow peas 3 minutes.

Spoon mixture on dinner dishes. Place snow peas in a pinwheel design around dish. Put olives between "spokes."

SERVES TWO

"SPAGHETTI & MEATBALLS"
SPAGHETTI

SPAGHETTI SQUASH, 2 lbs

Wash squash. Reserve a 2" slice off top for meatballs. Cut in half at center, then in half again from top to bottom. Don't peel. Steam 7 minutes with pulp side down.

"MEATBALLS"

1/3 cup GARBANZO BEANS	½ cup minced PARSLEY
1¼ cups WATER	½ cup peeled, finely grated
1 EGG YOLK	SPAGHETTI SQUASH
1 GARLIC clove, minced	½ cup BREAD CRUMBS
¼ cup minced ONION	2 tbsp VIRGIN OLIVE OIL
1 GARLIC clove, minced	

Soak garbanzo beans overnight in water. Refrigerate. After soaking, beans will expand to 1 cup.

Scramble egg in a bowl. Add onion, garlic and parsley. Grate beans in a good processor using a fine blade (an electric cheese grater will also work). Cut 2" off the top of the squash. Peel. Remove seeds and pulp. Grate. (It is crucial to the recipe that the beans and squash be grated finely.) Add both to bowl and mix. Add bread crumbs. Mix.

Shape mixture into 1" balls. Heat oil in skillet and fry 2 minutes on medium stirring occasionally. Turn off heat and leave on grate.

SAUCE

1 tbsp VIRGIN OLIVE OIL	4 PLUM TOMATOES, chopped
1 small ONION, chopped	½ cup chopped PARSLEY
1 GARLIC clove, minced	1 tbsp minced, fresh BASIL
3 large, ripe TOMATOES, liquefied	1 tbsp minced, fresh OREGANO

SERVES TWO

Remove meatballs from skillet. Heat oil. Add onions and garlic. Sauté 1 minute. Add remaining ingredients including meatballs. Simmer 5 minutes.

Squash: Use two forks, one to hold hot squash in place and the other to scrape "spaghetti" out onto a platter. Spoon into separate bowls. Pour sauce and "meatballs" over top. Sprinkle with parmesan cheese.

*This recipe requires overnight soaking of beans.

SPAGHETTI SQUASH & SPINACH SOUFFLÉ

½ of a medium SPAGHETTI SQUASH

1 bunch SPINACH, stems removed

¾ cup fresh PEAS

2 large TOMATOES, pureed

2 tbsp TOMATO PASTE, add to puree

4 medium PLUM TOMATOES, chopped

1¼ cups grated CHEDDAR CHEESE

Preheat broiler.

Slice squash 2" thick. Remove skins. Grate coarsely. Use a large steaming pot and steam 3 minutes. Add spinach and peas and steam 1 minute longer.

Remove steamer from pot. Turn off heat. Discard water.

Put all ingredients except ¼ cup of cheddar cheese in pot. Mix.

Transfer to greased baking dish. Sprinkle with remaining cheese.

Broil until cheese bubbles about 2 minutes.

SERVES TWO

FRIED GREEN TOMATOES & MUSHROOMS

2 tbsp SAFFLOWER OIL

3 medium GREEN TOMATOES, sliced

1 cup sliced MUSHROOMS

1 medium CARROT, grated

1 CELERY rib, slivered

1 cup chopped PARSLEY

½ tsp VEGETABLE SEASONING

¼ cup PINE NUTS

Heat oil in a large skillet. Sauté tomatoes, mushrooms, carrot and celery 4 minutes.
Add parsley and sauté 1 minute longer.
Add seasoning and nuts. Mix and serve.

TOMATOES, OKRA & MUSHROOMS

3 tbsp IMITATION BACON CHIPS

1 cup sliced OKRAS

1 cup sliced MUSHROOMS

6 large GREEN KALE leaves, halved,
  thinly sliced

2 tbsp BRAGG'S LIQUID AMINOS

2 tbsp BRAGG'S LIQUID
  AMINOS

1 CELERY rib, sliced

2 tbsp VIRGIN OLIVE OIL

1 GARLIC clove, minced

1½ cups chopped TOMATOES

Pour 1/3 cup hot water over bacon chips. Set aside.
Steam okras and mushrooms 4 minutes. Add kale and steam 1½ minutes longer.
Meantime liquefy aminos and celery in blender. Pour into small saucepan. Add olive oil, garlic and strained bacon chips. Simmer 1 minute.
Remove steamer from pot. Discard water. Put vegetables in pot including tomatoes and mix together. Scoop on to dinner dishes. Pour sauce over top.

SERVES TWO

CANDIED YAMS

3 pats BUTTER

3 tbsp MAPLE SYRUP

1 tbsp MOLASSES

3 tbsp ORANGE MARMALADE

3 cups julienned YAMS

1 medium-size PARSNIP,
  sliced

½ tsp GROUND CINNAMON

Melt butter in a small saucepan. Add syrup, molasses, marmalade. Heat on low.

Meantime steam yams and parsnip 3 minutes.

Place vegetables in soup bowls. Pour syrup over top. Sprinkle with cinnamon.

YAMS & GREENS

3 pats BUTTER

4 OKRAS, sliced

4 BRUSSELS SPROUTS, sliced

1 cup sliced SNOW PEAS

1½ cups julienned YAMS

Heat butter in large skillet. Add 3 tbsp water.

Cook okras and sprouts 3 minutes on medium-low heat. Keep pan cover on.

Add snow peas & yams and cook 2½ minutes.

This dish is so tasty, you don't need seasoning.

SERVES TWO

YAM & SPINACH PATTIES

½ cup OATMEAL

¼ cup WATER

2 cups grated YAMS

¼ cup finely diced CELERY center

1 bunch SPINACH, stems removed

1 CORN cob, kerneled

3 tbsp VIRGIN OLIVE OIL

Soak oatmeal with water while preparing food. Mix occasionally with a fork. Oatmeal should not be watery.

Use a large steamer and steam yams and celery 1½ minutes. Add spinach and steam 2½ minutes longer.

It's important to scrape cream off cob. Use a large bowl. Will be using this for mixing later. Add soaked oatmeal to corn and mix. Add vegetables and mix. Use two serrated knives and cut in a crisscross manner to separate and blend spinach with other vegetables.

Use a large serving spoon and drop mixture into a skillet set on medium-high. Push break-away foods into the patty or else they will burn. Fry 1 minute on each side. Lower heat. Fry 1 minute on each side.

YAMS, CORN & ALMOND BUTTER

3½ cups grated YAMS

1 CORN cob, kerneled

4 heaping tablespoon ALMOND BUTTER

1/4 to 1/3 cup WATER

SERVES TWO

Steam yams only 2 minutes. Any longer than that they will be mushy. If you are using frozen corn, add now.

Transfer to a small bowl and mix together. If using fresh corn, it is not necessary to cook. Be sure to scrape cream off cob with a paring knife.

Whip almond butter with distilled water in a nut chopper or blender. Make it the consistency of syrup.

Scoop mixture on dinner dishes. Pour almond syrup over top.

VARIATION: 1½ cups grated parsnips, and 2 cups grated yams. Use fresh peas instead of corn.

YAMS with PEACH MARMALADE

2 cups grated YAMS

1 medium PARSNIP, grated

1 tbsp MAPLE SYRUP or HONEY

1/3 cup PEACH PRESERVES

1/3 cup chopped ALMONDS

Steam yams and parsnips 2½ minutes.

Meantime combine syrup and preserves in a small saucepan. Stir while bringing to a simmer.

Put yams and parsnip in bowl. Add only half the almonds and mix. Transfer to dinner dishes. Pour marmalade sauce over top. Sprinkle with remaining almonds.

SERVES TWO

YAM & APPLE CASSEROLE

2 cups grated YAMS

1 yellow-skinned APPLE, seeded,
 sliced, cut in half

¾ cup APPLE JUICE

½ cup SUNFLOWER SEEDS

½ cup grated JICAMA

1 tsp ANISE

½ cup RAISINS (pour ¾ cups
 hot water over top and
 set aside)

Steam yams 2 minutes. Add apples. Remove from heat. Keep covered.

Put sunflower seeds in a nut chopper and grind to a meal. Put apple juice and sunflower meal in blender. Blend until smooth.

Combine yams, apples, jicama, anise, and drained raisins. Scoop into soup bowls. Spoon apple dressing over top.

YAMS & PARSNIP with PLUM SAUCE

Plum Sauce

1 tbsp LEMON JUICE

1 tbsp PIMENTOS, diced

¼ cup APPLESAUCE

1 PLUM, chopped

1 APRICOT, chopped

1 tbsp HONEY

Put all ingredients in the order given, except honey, in blender or nut chopper and chop. Put honey and sauce in a small saucepan and simmer 10 minutes stirring occasionally.

Vegetables

2 cups julienned YAMS

1 large PARSNIP, sliced thin

Steam yam and parsnip 2½ minutes before sauce is to be done.

Put vegetables in dish and pour sauce over top.

SERVES TWO

YAMS, SAVOY CABBAGE & CORN

3 cups thinly sliced SAVOY CABBAGE

1¾ cups grated YAMS

1 CORN cob, kerneled (don't scrape
  cream off yet)

½ tsp ANISE

½ cup chopped WALNUTS

3 tbsp WATER

    Steam cabbage 2 minutes. Add yams and steam 2 minutes longer.

    Add corn. Move from heat. Keep covered.

    Put walnuts in a nut chopper and grind to a meal. Add water and cream from corn, and swirl until creamy. Add more water if necessary.

    Transfer vegetables to · bowl and mix. Spoon onto dinner dishes. Pour nut dressing over top.

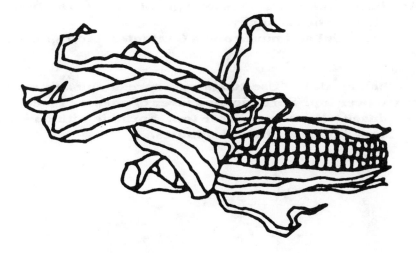

SERVES TWO

ZUCCHINI LASAGNA

1 tbsp VIRGIN OLIVE OIL

½ cup chipped ONION

1 large GARLIC clove, minced

4 cups chopped TOMATOES, pureed

2 tbsp TOMATO PASTE (puree with above)

4 PLUM TOMATOES, chopped

4 PARSLEY sprigs, chopped

1 tbsp minced, fresh BASIL leaves

1 tbsp minced, fresh OREGANO leaves

3 cups, sliced at a 45º angle, ZUCCHINI, (slice uniformly

1 cup sliced, large MUSHROOMS

1 bunch SPINACH, stems removed

1 cup grated MOZZARELLA CHEESE

Use a large skillet and heat oil. Sauté onion 1 minute. Add garlic and sauté 1 minute longer. Add both tomatoes and seasonings. Simmer partially covered while preparing rest of dish. Stir occasionally.

Meantime steam zucchini and mushrooms 6 minutes. Add spinach and steam 1 minute longer.

Preheat broiler.

Grease a large baking dish. Use tongs and spread spinach across bottom. Spoon half the sauce over top. Sprinkle on a layer of cheese. Place zucchini and mushrooms over spinach. Pour sauce over top. Sprinkle with cheese. Broil on lowest rack until cheese bubbles, about 2 minutes.

SERVES TWO

CABBAGE, RED PEPPER & CHINESE PEAS

1 tbsp VIRGIN OLIVE OIL

3 pats BUTTER

1 heaping soup bowlful
  sliced CABBAGE

¾ cup sliced OKRAS

1 RED BELL PEPPER, remove top,
  seeds and pulp. Slice

1 cup sliced CHINESE PEAS

2 SCALLIONS, sliced

¼ cup PINE NUTES (optional)

Heat oil and butter in large skillet on medium-low. Add vegetables in order given. Lower heat and sauté 3 minutes. Mix and sauté 2 minutes longer.

ZUCCHINI, SNOW PEAS & CORN

3 pats BUTTER

1½ cups sliced ZUCCHINI

1½ cups sliced SNOW PEAS

1 small ONION, chopped

1 large CORN cob, kerneled

1 tbsp minced BASIL (optional)

One 2 oz jar PIMENTOS

Melt butter in skillet. Sauté zucchini, snow peas and onion 4 minutes on medium-low.

Add corn, basil and pimentos. Turn off heat. Leave covered on hot grill 1 minute before serving.

SERVES TWO

ZUCCHINI, SPINACH & ROASTED PEPPERS

1 tbsp VIRGIN OLIVE OIL

2 pats BUTTER

2 medium ZUCCHINIS, sliced

1 large GARLIC clove, minced

2 tbsp BRAGG's LIQUID AMINOS

One 7 oz jar ROASTED
  PEPPERS

2 tbsp mild SALSA

1 large bunch SPINACH,
  stems removed

Use a large skillet and heat oil and butter. Sauté zucchini 2 minutes. Add garlic and sauté 1 minute longer. Add aminos, peppers and salsa. Simmer 2 minutes.
Meantime steam spinach 1½ minutes.
Use tongs to put spinach on dinner dishes. Spoon zucchini and sauce over top.

ZUCCHINI & SPINACH SOUFFLÉ

3 pats BUTTER

1 small ONION, halved, sliced

¾ cup sliced MUSHROOMS

½ can CREAM OF MUSHROOM SOUP

2½ cups sliced ZUCCHINI

1 bunch SPINACH, stems
  removed

¾ cup grated CHEDDAR
  CHEESE

PAPRIKA (optional)

Heat butter in a large pot. Sauté onion and mushrooms 2 minutes.
Add soup with 1/3 cup of water. Heat.
Add zucchini. Simmer 3 minutes. Add spinach. Simmer 1½ minutes.
Remove spinach with tongs onto a dinner plate. Chop. Combine with zucchini in a casserole. Add cheese. Mix gently.
Sprinkle with paprika.

SERVES TWO

ZUCCHINI & AVOCADOS with CARROTS

3 tbsp IMITATION BACON CHIPS

3 cups sliced ZUCCHINI

1½ cups sliced CARROT

¼ cup chopped CHIVES

2 tbsp BRAGG'S LIQUID AMINOS

1 tbsp VIRGIN OLIVE OIL

¾ cup chopped ZUCCHINI

1 GARLIC clove, minced

2 HAAS AVOCADOS

Soak bacon chips in 1/3 cups hot water. Set aside.

Steam zucchini, carrot and chives 3 minutes.

Meantime combine aminos, oil, chopped zucchini and garlic in blender and liquefy. Remove glass from stand. Add drained bacon chips. Mix with a wooden spoon. Simmer 2 minutes in small saucepan.

Cut avocado in half. Remove pit. Cut thin slices in both directions while still in skin. Set aside.

Spoon steamed vegetables on dinner dishes. Spoon and scatter avocado over vegetables. Pour sauce over top.

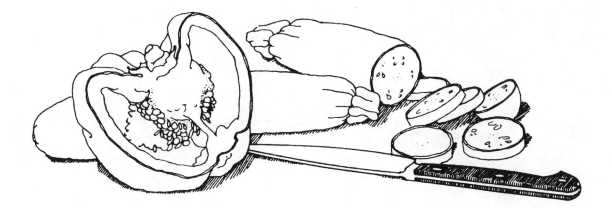

SERVES TWO

110

Notes

VEGETABLE
GRAINS & LEGUMES ENTREÉS

HEALTH & NUTRITION
Guide for GRAINS and LEGUMES;

BUYING LEGUMES

When purchasing legumes, check closely for uniformity in size, and depth and clarity of color. Unevenness of size may create a dish that is unevenly cooked. Fading color indicates that the warehouse storage time was probably too long. When beans and peas are shriveled, cracked, pocked by insects, or when packages contain rocks or other materials, it is an indication of a low quality product.

STORING LEGUMES

It is advisable to store all dry legumes in tightly covered, clear glass or plastic containers away from heat and moisture. Add 2 bay leaves to each container to prevent the invasion of insects.

NUTRITIONAL INFORMATION

Legumes are a superb source of high-quality protein. Most dried beans and peas contain an average of 17 to 25 percent aminos acids, which is approximately double the amount found in other vegetable and animal sources. Soybeans rate highest, with a total aminos base of 38 percent. Combining any dried legume with one or more of any whole grain or cereal ensures a complete protein meal. Most legumes are extra ordinarily low in fat and are an excellent source of calcium, iron and B-vitamins. They are especially high in B-1, thiamine and niacin. When sprouted, nature miraculously increases the total vitamin content and amazingly creates the addition of vitamin C in each tender little shoot.

INSTRUCTIONS FOR PREPARING AND COOKING GRAINS AND LEGUMES

ALL the GRAINS and LEGUMES in the ingredients are **UNCOOKED**. They must be **SOAKED OVERNIGHT** in **DISTILLED WATER**. **REFRIGERATE** to prevent fermentation.

Prior to cooking, dried legumes should be carefully picked over, removing any stones or other foreign debris. Discard beans that are flat or float in water, wash thoroughly, and place in a large bowl. Dried beans of all types should be soaked in cold water to rehydrate them. Because they swell during this process, cover them with at least twice their volume of water. Soak for 6 to 8 hours. All of the soaking liquid should be retained and used in the cooking process when the recipe calls for using water. Soybeans are the exception; the original water must be discarded and replaced with fresh water before cooking.

You will see how quick and easy it is to use grains in your meals by soaking grains and legumes. You might keep several jars soaking in the refrigerator in case you forget to put one in the night before. I suggest using them within a week, and after the second day, change the water.

Do not add salt when beans are cooking. It slows the cooking process, and can even prevent the beans from softening.

How to Soak Garbanzo Beans
(also known as Chick Peas)

Place dry garbanzo beans in a wide-mouth jar or covered casserole dish. Use a proportion of one part beans to three parts water. The beans will triple in size. Always use drinking or distilled water. Refrigerate. If using a jar, shake the container occasionally. Shaking prevents the beans from pressing against each other when they swell making it difficult to remove them. Rinse and change the water after the first day. For best results, soak them for two days.

CHARACTERISTIC

Adzuki Beans: Delicate in flavor, this tiny deep-red bean is known in the Orient as the "King of Beans." Easiest of all legumes to assimilate, it is a delicious addition to almost any dish requiring beans.

Black Beans: A member of the kidney bean family. They have a rich earthy flavor and are commonly used in soups and stews.

Black-eyed Peas: Also known as china beans, cow peas or black-eyed beans.

Chick-Peas (Garbanzo Beans): Widely used in international cuisine. Their delightfully nutty flavor is a wonderful addition to pates, salads, soups or stews or bakes in casseroles.

Lima Beans: Savory and distinctive in taste, red beans are wonderful when combined with rice or used as a substitute in dishes calling for pinto beans.

Soybeans: Since ancient times, this small hard bean known by people of the Far East as the "meat of the earth." The incredible versatile soybean provides a variety of products, such as, flour, oil, milk, tofu, tempeh and miso. Soy beans are used in spicy pates, salads and casseroles.

Split Peas: Split peas are dried peas without skins and cook very quickly. They are most often used in vegetarian and meat-based soups.

White or Great Northern Bean: Also known as navy beans, (pea beans). These tasty morsels keep their shape and taste best when slowly simmered or baked.

AVOCADO, CORN & BARLEY

¾ cup uncooked PURLED BARLEY

1 tbsp VIRGIN OLIVE OIL

2 pats BUTTER

1 large GARLIC clove, minced

1 CORN cob, kerneled

2 tbsp CHOPPED BLACK OLIVES

2 tbsp diced PIMENTO

2 large HAAS AVOCADOS

Soak barley overnight in 1½ cups distilled water. Refrigerate. When preparing meal drain barley well.

Heat oil and butter in a skillet. Sauté barley 4 minutes. Add garlic and sauté 1 minute longer. Add corn and olives and turn off heat. Leave covered on hot grate 1 minute.

Remove seed from avocado and spoon out of skin. Cut each half in quarters, lengthwise. Place on dishes in a star design. Pour barley mixture over top. Sprinkle with pimentos.

STRING BEANS, BARLEY & RED BELL PEPPER

1 tbsp VIRGIN OLIVE OIL

3 pats BUTTER

¾ cup uncooked PURLED BARLEY

2 cup slivered STRING BEANS

1 RED BELL PEPPER, halved, pulp and seeds removed, thinly sliced

1 package dry ONION SOUP

2/3 cup WATER

Soak barley overnight in 1½ cups distilled water. When preparing meal drain well.

Melt butter in a large skillet. Sauté barley, string beans, and pepper 3 minutes on medium-low.

Mix soup and water. Add to skillet. Mix. Raise heat ½ minute. Return to medium-low and simmer 2 minutes.

SERVES TWO

SWEET-AND-SOUR BEANS

½ cup BABY NAVY BEANS

3 tbsp IMITATION BACON CHIPS

1 small ONION, chopped

¾ cup CELERY slivers

1 GARLIC clove, minced

2 tbsp SAFFLOWER OIL

½ can TOMATO PASTE

½ tsp CHILI SEASONING MIX

2 tbsp MOLASSES

1/3 cup chopped PINEAPPLE CHUNKS

2 tbsp SWEET RELISH

Soak beans overnight in 1¼ cups distilled water. When preparing meal drain well.

Cover bacon chips with 1/3 cup hot water. Set aside.

Bring 1 cup water to boil. Add beans. Simmer covered 5 minutes.

Two minutes before beans are done, heat oil in a large skillet and sauté onion. celery and garlic 2 minutes.

Add beans and cooking water, tomato paste, chile seasoning, molasses and bacon chips. Simmer 5 minutes.

Add pineapple and relish. Turn off heat. Leave on hot grill 1 minute.

BEETS, BARLEY & APPLES

½ cup uncooked PURLED BARLEY

2 medium BEETS, peeled, sliced

1 large, yellow, sweet APPLE, halved, sliced

1/3 cup RAISINS

¼ tsp powdered CLOVES

1/3 cup slivered ALMONDS

Soak barley overnight in 1¼ cups distilled water. Soak raisins in ¾ cup water. Refrigerate. When preparing meal drain both well.

Steam beets and barley (beets on bottom) 6 minutes. Add apples and raisins. Steam 1 more minute longer.

Place beets and barley on dinner dishes. Scoop apples and raisins over top. Season. Sprinkle with almonds.

SERVES TWO

HARVARD BEETS, NAVY BEANS & BRUSSELS SPROUTS

½ cup uncooked NAVY BEANS

2 tbsp fresh LEMON JUICE

1 tbsp chopped SWEET PICKLES

3 pats BUTTER

2 tbsp HONEY

1 tbsp MOLASSES

2 medium-size fresh BEETS, quartered, sliced thin

BEET GREENS, stems removed, chopped

5 large BRUSSELS SPROUTS, thinly sliced

Soak navy beans overnight in 1¼ cups distilled water. Refrigerate. When ready to prepare meal drain well.

Use a double boiler. After water boils add lemon juice, pickles, butter, honey and molasses. Simmer until ready to use.

Steam beans 4 minutes. Add beets and steam 2 minutes longer. Add sprouts and steam 3 minutes. Add beet greens and steam 1 minute. Remove steamer from pot. Discard water. Return vegetables to pot. Add sauce. Mix and serve.

Beans that haven't absorbed the red from beets, have not softened in the soaking process. Discard them.

BEETS, BARLEY & PEAS

½ cup uncooked PURLED BARLEY

3 pats BUTTER

2 medium BEETS, peeled, halved, sliced

¾ cup fresh PEAS

1 cup peeled, chopped ZUCCHINI, liquefied

¼ tsp powdered CLOVES

SERVES TWO

Soak barley overnight in 1¼ cups distilled water. When preparing meal drain well.

Heat butter in a 3-qt. saucepan. Sauté barley on low heat 5 minutes.

Meantime steam beets 6 minutes. Add peas. Turn off heat. Keep covered on hot grate 1 minute.

Add zucchini and seasoning to barley. Heat. Scoop vegetables on dinner dishes. Spoon barley and sauce over top.

BROCCOLI & BARLEY with TOMATO

1 cup uncooked PURLED BARLEY

3 pats BUTTER

1 small ONION, chopped

2 cups BROCCOLI florets

2 BOK CHOY LEAVES, keep stems and leaves separate. Cut length-wise, sliver

1 tbsp SAFFLOWER OIL

2 tbsp BRAGG'S LIQUID AMINOS

3 tbsp KETCHUP

2 medium TOMATOES, chopped

½ tsp DEHYDRATED VEGETABLE SEASONING

Soak barley in 1¼ cups distilled water overnight. Refrigerate. When preparing meal drain well.

Steam broccoli and bok choy stems 4 minutes. Add leaves and steam 2 minutes longer.

Meantime, sauté barley and onion in butter 4 minutes in a skillet.

Use a small saucepan and combine oil, aminos and ketchup. Simmer. Remove from heat. Add wine.

Put broccoli, bok choy and barley in a bowl. Stir in sauce and tomatoes. Mix.

SERVES TWO

RED CABBAGE, KALE AND NAVY BEANS

½ cup uncooked NAVY BEANS

3 tbsp IMITATION BACON CHIPS

6 cups thinly sliced RED CABBAGE

small bunch smooth KALE

1 tbsp VIRGIN OLIVE OIL

3 pats BUTTER

1 large GARLIC clove, minced

1 tbsp minced fresh BASIL

Soak navy beans overnight in 1¼ cups distilled water. Refrigerate. When ready to prepare meal drain well.

Pour 1/3 cup hot water over bacon chips. Set aside.

Steam beans 5 minutes. Add red cabbage and steam 3 minutes longer. Add kale and steam 2 minutes.

Meantime heat oil and butter in a small saucepan. Sauté garlic 3 minutes.

Remove steamer from pot. Cover vegetables. Discard water.

Return vegetables to pot. Add butter sauce and strained bacon chips. Mix.

GARBANZO STUFFED CABBAGE ROLLS

½ cup uncooked GARBANZO BEANS

1½ cups DISTILLED WATER

2 tbsp VIRGIN OLIVE OIL

2 pats BUTTER

¾ cup diced CELERY rib

1/3 cup chopped SCALLIONS

1 tbsp dry ONION SOUP

¼ cup WATER

¾ cup chopped PARSLEY

1½ cups chopped TOMATOES, liquefied

3 tbsp dry ONION SOUP

4 large or 6 small outer CABBAGE LEAVES

SERVES TWO

Soak beans overnight in distilled water. Refrigerate. When preparing meal drain well. Grind in a food processor using coarse blade. An electric grater will work.

Heat oil and butter in a skillet on medium-high. Sauté beans 3 minutes stirring several times. Lower heat. Add celery and scallions. Sauté 2 minutes. Add onion soup (dump soup into small saucer and mix until evenly blended.), water and parsley. Turn heat down to low. Keep covered.

Pour liquefied tomatoes into small saucepan with onion soup. Simmer 3 minutes. Keep covered.

Meantime score raised side of stem on cabbage so it will roll. Steam cabbage 3 to 4 minutes until soft.

Remove all cabbage leaves with tongs onto each dinner dish. Spoon mixture evenly on cabbage leaves. Roll. Pour tomato sauce over cabbage.

KIDNEY BEANS, SAVOY CABBAGE & CORN

3 tbsp IMITATION BACON CHIPS

½ cup uncooked RED KIDNEY BEANS

6 cups sliced SAVOY CABBAGE

1 CORN cob, kerneled

1 tbsp BRAGG'S LIQUID AMINOS

1 tbsp SAFFLOWER OIL

1 large CELERY rib, chopped

Pour ½ cup hot water over bacon chips. Set aside.

Soak beans overnight in 1½ cup distilled water. When preparing meal drain well.

Steam beans 5 minutes. Add cabbage and steam 3 minutes longer.

Meantime put aminos, oil and celery in a blender and liquefy. Add strained bacon chips. Mix with a wooden spoon.

Remove steamer from pot. Discard water. Add liquid mixture, beans, cabbage and corn. Heat slightly while mixing.

SERVES TWO

CABBAGE & LIMA BEANS with AVOCADO

½ cup uncooked LIMA BEANS

3 tbsp IMITATION BACON CHIPS

6 cups sliced CABBAGE

1 medium CARROT, grated

½ cup chopped PARSLEY

2 tbsp BRAGG'S LIQUID AMINOS

1 medium ZUCCHINI, peeled
  chopped

1 large AVOCADO

Soak beans overnight in 1½ cup distilled water. Refrigerate. When preparing meal drain well.

Pour 1/3 cup hot water over bacon chips. Set aside.

Steam beans 6 minutes. Add cabbage and steam 2 minutes longer. Add carrots and parsley and steam 2 minutes.

Meantime put aminos and zucchini in a blender. Cut avocado in half. Remove pit. Take on half, and spoon chunks into blender. Get a good grip on the glass and base, and rock back and forth until the solids have blended.

Take other half of avocado. Slice thin lines horizontally and vertically while still in skin. Set aside.

Remove vegetables from steamer. Put in mixing bowl and mix. Spoon in sliced avocado. Mix gently.

Scoop onto dinner dishes and pour dressing over top. Sprinkle with strained bacon chips.

KALE, GARBANZO & ROASTED PEPPERS

½ cup uncooked GARBANZO BEANS

1 bunch KALE, stems removed, chopped

½ cup WATER

2 pats BUTTER

One 2 oz package dry ONION SOUP

One 7 oz jar ROASTED PEPPERS
  chopped

SERVES TWO

Soak garbanzo beans in 1½ cups distilled water overnight. Refrigerate. When preparing meal drain well.

Steam garbanzo beans 6 minutes. Add kale and steam 1½ minutes longer.

Remove steamer from pot. Cover vegetables to keep warm. Discard.

Heat water and add butter. Add onion soup. Simmer ½ minute. Stir in steamed vegetables.

Spoon onto dinner dishes. Sprinkle with peppers.

CHICKPEA PATTIES

1/3 cup uncooked CHICKPEAS (also called GARBANZO BEANS)

3 tbsp IMITATION BACON CHIPS

1½ cups grated CARROTS

¼ cup diced ONION

¼ cup diced CELERY

¼ cup chopped PARSLEY

1 EGG

½ cup BREAD CRUMBS

3 tbsp VIRGIN OLIVE OIL

Soak chickpeas overnight in 1½ cups distilled water. Refrigerate. When preparing meal drain well.

Soak bacon chips with 1/3 cup hot water. Set aside.

Steam carrots, onion and celery 1½ minutes.

Grate chickpeas in food processor using fine grater. An electric grater would also work.

Scramble egg in a large bowl. Add steamed vegetables and parsley. Mix. Add grated chick peas and strained bacon chips. Mix. Gradually add bread crumbs until the mixture can be formed into patties.

Heat oil on a medium-high heat. Fry patties 1 minute on each side. Keep pan covered. Lower heat to medium-low and fry 1 minute longer on each side.

Serve with sliced tomatoes and cucumber spears.

SERVES TWO

LIMA BEANS, CARROTS & KALE

½ cup LIMA BEANS

1½ cups grated CARROT

1 medium bunch KALE, stems removed, chopped

½ cup WATER

3 pats BUTTER

1 package ONION SOUP MIX

1 tsp VEGETABLE SEASONING

Soak lima beans overnight in 1½ cups distilled water. When ready to prepare meal drain well.

Use a large pot and steam beans 6 minutes. Add carrot, kale and onion and steam 2 minutes longer.

Remove steamer from pot. Cover vegetables to keep warm. Heat water and butter. Add onion soup mix.

Add beans and vegetables. Mix.

LENTILS, CARROTS & OKRAS

1/3 cup uncooked LENTILS

1 tbsp VIRGIN OLIVE OIL

2 pats BUTTER

1½ cups grated CARROTS

1 cup sliced OKRA

1 large GARLIC CLOVE, minced

½ cup chopped PARSLEY

1 tbsp BRAGG's LIQUID AMINOS

¾ cup peeled, chopped ZUCCHINI

Soak lima beans overnight in 1½ cups water. When ready to prepare meal drain well.

Heat oil and butter on medium-low in a large skillet. Sauté beans 3 minutes.

Add okra and sauté 3 minutes longer. Add carrots, garlic and parsley. Sauté 1½ minutes.

Meantime put aminos and zucchini in blender and liquefy. Add to vegetables. Heat.

SERVES TWO

CAULIFLOWER with BEAN SAUCE

½ cup uncooked RED KIDNEY BEANS

2 cups CAULIFLOWER florets

¾ cup grated ZUCCHINI

½ cup chopped CELERY

3 pats BUTTER

1 GARLIC clove, minced

1 CORN cob, kerneled

Soak beans overnight in 1½ cups distilled water. Refrigerate. When preparing meal drain well.

Steam cauliflower 6 minutes. Add zucchini and steam 1 minute longer.

Meantime simmer beans in 1 cup of the soaking water 5 minutes. Keep covered. Mix beans occasionally by holding onto the handle and lid, and gently swirl the pot. Put celery, beans, ½ cup of the cooking water, butter and garlic in blender. Blend to a creamy consistency. Add more water if necessary.

Spread cauliflower on dinner dishes. Sprinkle with zucchini and corn. Spoon bean sauce over top.

SERVES TWO

BLACK BEANS & CAULIFLOWER

1/3 cup uncooked BLACK BEANS	1½ cups peeled, chopped ZUCCHINI
3 cups CAULIFLOWER florets	3 tbsp WATER
1 bunch GREEN KALE	3 pats BUTTER
½ cup chopped CELERY	½ tsp VEGETABLE SEASONING

Soak beans in 1½ cups distilled water overnight. Refrigerate. When preparing meal drain well. Simmer in 1 cup of the soaking water 5 minutes. Keep covered. Mix beans occasionally getting a firm grip on the handle and hold the lid down. Gently swirl the pot.

Meantime steam cauliflower 5 minutes. Add kale and steam 1½ minutes longer.

Put celery and zucchini in blender and blend until creamy. Melt butter in small saucepan. Add celery/zucchini mixture. Put water in blender and swirl to remove residual. Add to saucepan with seasoning. Simmer.

Remove kale with tongs and spread on dinner dishes. Layer cauliflower over kale. Pour sauce over top. Sprinkle with corn and beans.

STUFFED GRAPE LEAVES

1/3 cup uncooked PURLED BARLEY	¾ cup grated CARROT or YAM
¼ cup CURRANTS (Soak in ½ cup hot water 4 minutes)	¼ cup chopped PARSLEY
	1 small CORN cob, kerneled
3 tbsp VIRGIN OLIVE OIL	¼ cup PINE NUTS
2 pats BUTTER	12 fresh or bottled GRAPE LEAVES

SERVES TWO

Sauce

2 tbsp VIRGIN OLIVE OIL

2 tbsp LIME JUICE

3 tbsp DRY WHITE WINE

1 tbsp fresh, minced BASIL

Soak barley in 1½ cups water overnight. Refrigerate. When preparing meal drain well.

Bring 2 cups of water to a boil.

Heat oil and butter in a large skillet on medium-low. Sauté barley 4 minutes. Do not cook on too high a heat or barley will get crunchy and hard. Add carrots and sauté 2½ minutes longer. Add parsley, currants, corn, and pine nuts and sauté 1 minute.

Meantime, if using bottled grape leaves, scald with 2 cups of hot water in a bowl and drain into a colander. If you have never used bottled grape leaves before, they are tightly rolled up in one roll, and pushed snugly in a bottle. Use tongs to get them out. A few might be damaged but there's more than enough to use.

If using fresh leaves drop young pale-green leaves into boiling water and blanch till color darkens - about 4 to 5 minutes. Drain on a rack.

Snip off stems of either fresh or bottled leaves.

Pat dry grape leaves with a dish towel. Put shiny surface down on a board. Use a spoon and set the stuffing near the broad end of the leaf and fold over the left and right segments. Then roll the enclosed ball toward the leaf-tip. Place the packet loose side down in the skillet. Use toothpicks if you prefer.

Combine oil, juice and basil in a cup. Pour sauce over top. Simmer on low 2 minutes.

SERVES TWO

BARLEY & GREENS

¾ cup uncooked PURLED BARLEY

3 pats BUTTER

¾ cup sliced OKRAS

4 large BRUSSELS SPROUTS, sliced

1 cup sliced CHINESE PEAS

1 CELERY rib, slivered

¼ cup chopped PARSLEY

¼ tsp VEGETABLE SEASONING

Soak barley in 1 ½ cups distilled water overnight. Refrigerate. When preparing meal drain well.

Melt butter in large skillet. Add 3 tbsp water.

Add barley, okras, and sprouts. Cook on low 4 minutes. Add peas, celery and parsley and cook 3 minutes longer. Season.

OATMEAL BURGERS

¾ cup OATMEAL

½ cup DRINKING WATER

½ cup finely grated CARROTS

1/3 cup finely chopped GREEN PEPPER

¼ cup minced ONION

½ cup diced, tender center CELERY rib

¾ cup, coarsely ground
  SUNFLOWER SPROUTS

¼ cup minced PARSLEY

SALAD GREENS

2 tbsp VIRGIN OLIVE OIL

medium TOMATO, sliced

Soak oatmeal in water 5 minutes. This mixture should be moist, not watery. Mix with fork occasionally.

Meantime steam carrots, peppers, celery and onion 2 minutes. Combine with oats and parsley. Mix. Add sunflower sprouts. Mix thoroughly. Shape into patties.

Heat oil in a large skillet. Fry patties on medium-high 1 minute on each side. Lower heat and cook 2 minutes on each side.

Make a bed of greens. Place patties on top. Garnish with tomato.

SERVES TWO

ORIENTAL BARLEY CASSEROLE

½ cup uncooked PURLED BARLEY

1 tbsp SAFFLOWER OIL

3 pats BUTTER

½ cup sliced MUSHROOMS

1 cup slivered SNOW PEAS

1½ cups finely sliced SAVOY CABBAGE

½ cup chopped SCALLIONS

½ cup CELERY slivers

½ tsp grated, fresh GINGER

3 tbsp BRAGG's LIQUID
  AMINOS

1/3 cup slivered ALMONDS

Soak barley overnight in 1½ cups distilled water. Refrigerate. When preparing meal, drain well.

Heat oil and butter in skillet on medium-low. Sauté all ingredients except aminos and almonds 3 minutes. Lower heat. Add aminos and simmer 4 minutes longer.

Sprinkle with almonds when served.

SERVES TWO

BARLEY, PEAS & MUSHROOMS

¾ cup uncooked PURLED BARLEY

1 tbsp SAFFLOWER OIL

3 pats BUTTER

¾ cup sliced MUSHROOMS

1/3 cup CELERY slivers

2 tbsp BRAGG's LIQUID AMINOS

1¼ cups peeled, chopped
 ZUCCHINI

2 tbsp WATER

1 cup fresh PEAS

Soak barley overnight in 1½ cups distilled water. Refrigerate. When preparing meal, drain well.

Heat oil and butter in large skillet on medium-low. Sauté barley 2 minutes. Lower heat. (Too high of a heat will make barley crunchy.) Add mushrooms and celery. Sauté 4 minutes longer.

Put aminos and zucchini in blender and blend until creamy. Stir into skillet. Add water to blender and swirl to remove residual. Add to skillet. Simmer 2 minutes.

Add peas. Simmer ½ minute.

CHILI BEANS with GREEN PEPPER

½ cup uncooked RED KIDNEY BEANS

1½ cups WATER

½ cup ELBOW MACARONI

2 tbsp VIRGIN OLIVE OIL

1 small ONION, chopped

¼ cup CELERY slivers

¾ cup diced GREEN BELL PEPPER

1 GARLIC CLOVE, minced

3 cups chopped TOMATOES,
 liquefied

2 tbsp TOMATO PASTE

1 tsp CHILI SEASONING MIX

2 PLUM TOMATOES, chopped
 small

SERVES TWO

Soak kidney beans overnight in 1½ cups distilled water. When preparing meal, drain well.

Follow directions on package to cook macaroni.

Meantime heat oil in a large skillet. Sauté beans, onion, celery, and pepper 3 minutes. Add garlic and sauté 1 minute longer.

Stir in liquefied tomatoes, tomato paste and seasoning. Simmer 5 minutes.

Stir in plum tomatoes and macaroni. Simmer 1 minute.

STUFFED PEPPER with BEAN DIP

½ cup uncooked RED KIDNEY BEANS

¾ cup grated PARSNIP

½ cup finely grated CARROT

1/3 cup chopped ONIONS

2 GREEN BELL PEPPERS, seeds and pulp

  removed, cut from bottom to top

½ cup chopped CELERY

3 pats BUTTER

1 CORN cob, kerneled

Soak beans overnight in 1½ cups distilled water. Refrigerate. When preparing meal, drain well. Simmer beans in 1 cup of the soaking water. Keep covered. Mix beans occasionally by holding on to the handle and lid, and gently swirl the pot.

Meantime layer parsnip, carrot, onions and peppers in a steamer, and steam 3 minutes.

Put celery, beans, 1½ cup of the cooking water, and butter in a blender. Blend until syrupy. Add more water if necessary.

Remove peppers and put in a covered casserole.

Put remaining vegetables in a bowl. Stir in bean mixture. Spoon into peppers.

SERVES TWO

GREEN PEPPER & KIDNEY BEANS

½ cup uncooked KIDNEY BEANS

2 GREEN PEPPERS

1 tbsp VIRGIN OLIVE OIL

1 SCALLION, sliced

1 GARLIC CLOVE minced

3 large TOMATOES, quartered

2 tbsp TOMATO PASTE

1 tbsp minced, fresh BASIL

3 tbsp mild SALSA

1 medium ZUCCHINI, coarsely grated

2 PLUM TOMATOES, chopped

Soak kidney beans overnight in 1½ cup distilled water. Refrigerate. When preparing meal drain well. Note: Not all beans swell during the soaking process. Remove any small, red, shiny beans now.

Heat oil and butter in a 3-qt. saucepan. Sauté beans 4 minutes.

Add scallions and garlic and sauté 1 minute.

Cut pepper from bottom to top. Remove seeds and pulp. The peppers are to lie sideways.

Liquefy large tomatoes and tomato paste in blender. Add to sauce pan with basil and salsa. Simmer 4 minutes.

Add zucchini and plum tomatoes. Simmer 1 minute.

Place peppers on a dinner dish. Spoon mixture over peppers.

STUFFED PEPPERS with BARLEY

¾ cup uncooked PURLED BARLEY

2 large green BELL PEPPERS, slice from bottom to top. Keep stem on. Remove seeds and pulp.

3 pats BUTTER

3 OKRAS, sliced

3 tbsp minced, fresh BASIL LEAVES

1 CORN cob, kerneled

3 PLUM TOMATOES, diced

2 tbsp mild SALSA

2 medium-large TOMATOES, chopped

SERVES TWO

Soak barley in 1½ cups distilled water overnight. Refrigerate. When preparing meal drain well.

Steam peppers 3 minutes.

Meantime sauté barley and okra in butter 4 minutes on medium low. High heat will cause the barley to get crunchy and hard. Add basil, corn, tomato and salsa. Sauté 1 minute longer.

Puree tomatoes in blender with tomato paste. Add to mixture. Simmer 3 minutes.

Scoop mixture into peppers using a slotted spoon. Pour sauce over top.

SPINACH, BARLEY & BEETS

¾ cup uncooked PURLED BARLEY

2 medium-large BEETS, peeled, julienned

1 tsp SAFFLOWER OIL

3 pats BUTTER

½ cup chopped ONION

1 bunch SPINACH, stems removed

1½ cups peeled, chopped ZUCCHINI

2 tbsp BRAGG's LIQUID AMINOS

2 tbsp WATER

¼ tsp DILL SEED

¼ cup sliced BLACK OLIVES

Soak barley in 1½ cups distilled water overnight. Refrigerate. When preparing meal drain well.

Steam beets 7 minutes. Add spinach and steam 1 minute longer (Might have to add more water to steamer).

Meantime heat oil and butter in a skillet. Sauté barley 5 minutes. Add onion and sauté 2 minutes longer.

Liquefy zucchini with aminos and water. Add to barley with dill seed. Simmer 2 minutes.

Remove spinach with tongs and spread on dinner dishes. Place beets on top. Spoon barley mixture over top in the shape of an "X". Sprinkle with olives.

SERVES TWO

LENTILS, SPINACH & BUTTERNUT SQUASH

1/3 cup uncooked LENTILS

1 tbsp VIRGIN OLIVE OIL

3 pats BUTTER

2 cups grated BUTTERNUT SQUASH*

1 bunch SPINACH, stems removed

½ cup CREAM OF MUSHROOM
SOUP

1/3 cup WATER

Soak lentils overnight in 1½ cups distilled water. Refrigerate. When ready to prepare meal drain well.

Heat oil and butter in a skillet on medium-low. Sauté lentils 4 minutes.

Meantime slice squash 2" thick. Remove skin. Scrape out seeds and pulp. Grate. Add to skillet and sauté 4 minutes longer.

Steam spinach 1 minute. Remove from steamer with tongs onto a platter. Slice into small pieces.

Add in separate sections to skillet and mix.

Heat soup and water in a small saucepan.

Spoon vegetable mixture on dinner dishes. Pour sauce over top.

SPLIT PEAS, SPAGHETTI SQUASH & CARROTS

½ cup uncooked SPLIT PEAS

1 tbsp VIRGIN OLIVE OIL

2 pats BUTTER

2½ cups grated SPAGHETTI SQUASH

¾ cup grated CARROT

2 pats BUTTER

1 GARLIC clove, minced

½ can PEA SOUP

1/3 cup WATER

SERVES TWO

Soak split peas overnight in 1½ cups distilled water. Refrigerate. When ready to prepare meal drain well.

Heat oil and butter in a skillet on medium-low. Sauté peas 4 minutes. Raise heat to medium-high. Add squash and carrot and sauté 3 minutes longer.

Meantime melt butter in a small saucepan. Sauté garlic 1 minute. Add pea soup and water. Heat.

Place vegetables on dinner dishes. Pour sauce over top.

SERVES TWO

Notes

VEGETABLE/PASTA ENTREÉS

ARTICHOKE HEARTS & NOODLES with HERB SAUCE

3 pats BUTTER

1 tbsp VIRGIN OLIVE OIL

1 small ONION, diced

1 GARLIC clove, minced

2 tbsp BRAGG's LIQUID AMINOS

1 large unpeeled ZUCCHINI, chopped small

1/3 cup WATER

1 tbsp minced, fresh BASIL

1 tbsp minced, fresh OREGANO

¼ tsp DILL SEED

1 medium CARROT, peeled, grated

1 cup chopped fresh PARSLEY

1 cup ARTICHOKE HEARTS in water (buy 14-oz jar)

½ cup fresh PEAS

PARMESAN CHEESE

Cook noodles following directions on package.

Heat butter and oil in a 3-qt. saucepan. Sauté onion 2 minutes. Add garlic and sauté 1 minute longer.

Put aminos and zucchini in blender and liquefy. Add to saucepan. Pour water in blender. Swirl to remove residual zucchini. Add to saucepan. Add basil, oregano and dill seed. Simmer.

Add carrot and parsley. Simmer 3 minutes. Keep covered.

Drain artichokes by shaking back and fourth in a hand-held strainer. Cut in half from stem to top. Add to saucepan. Simmer 1 minute. Add peas. Simmer ½ minute.

Spread noodles on dinner dish. Pour mixture over top. Sprinkle with cheese.

SERVES TWO

ASPARAGUS, CORN & PASTA

½ cup uncooked ELBOW MACARONI

¾ lb ASPARAGUS, sliced

2 tbsp SAFFLOWER OIL

3 tbsp BRAGG'S LIQUID AMINOS

3 tbsp mild, fresh SALSA

2 tbsp TOMATO PASTE

¼ cup WATER

1 GARLIC clove, minced

1 CORN cob, kerneled

Follow directions on package to cook macaroni.

Steam asparagus 5 minutes.

Meantime put oil, aminos, salsa, tomato paste, water and garlic in a small saucepan and simmer 5 minutes. Add water if necessary.

Combine macaroni, asparagus and corn in a bowl. Spoon on dinner dishes. Pour sauce over top.

BEETS, PASTA & SPINACH

½ cup uncooked ELBOW MACARONI

2 medium BEETS, julienned or sliced thin

BEET GREENS, stems removed, chopped (if not
 using fresh beets, replace with other greens)

2 tbsp BRAGG'S LIQUID AMINOS

1 cup peeled, chopped
 ZUCCHINI

3 pats BUTTER

1 GARLIC clove, minced

Cook macaroni following directions on package.

Meantime steam beets 6 minutes in a large steamer. Add spinach. Steam 1 minute longer. Put aminos and zucchini in blender and liquefy.

Remove steamer from pot. Cover vegetables to keep warm. Discard water. Melt butter. Sauté garlic 1 minute. Add zucchini and heat.

Combine beets, spinach and macaroni. Scoop onto dinner dishes. Pour sauce over top.

SERVES TWO

PASTA, BROCCOLI & CORN

½ cup uncooked ELBOW MACARONI

3 cups BROCCOLI florets

1 large RED BELL PEPPER, diced

½ can CREAM OF ONION SOUP

1/3 cup WATER

2 tbsp fresh CHIVES, minced

Cook macaroni following directions on package.
Meantime steam broccoli and pepper 4 minutes.
Remove steamer from pot. Cover vegetables to keep warm. Discard water.
Pour soup in pot. Add 1/3 cup water and chives. Heat. Add macaroni, broccoli and pepper. Mix.

PASTA, BROCCOLI & WALNUTS

½ cup uncooked ELBOW MACARONI

3 cups BROCCOLI florets

1 CELERY rib, slivered

2 medium TOMATOES, chopped small

½ tsp VEGETABLE SEASONING

½ cup chopped WALNUTS

Cook macaroni following direction son package.
Meantime steam broccoli and celery 5 minutes.
Put tomatoes, seasoning and walnuts in large bowl. Add broccoli and celery.
Mix. Add macaroni and mix.

SERVES TWO

CHARD & PASTA with CHEDDAR SAUCE

½ cup uncooked ELBOW MACARONI

3 pats BUTTER

1 tbsp WHOLE WHEAT FLOUR

¾ cup MILK

¾ cup shredded SHARP CHEDDAR CHEESE

¼ tsp WORCESTERSHIRE SAUCE

1½ cups chopped RED BELL PEPPER

½ cup chopped ONION

1½ lbs CHARD, stems removed chopped

½ tsp VEGETABLE SEASONING

Cook macaroni following directions on package.

In a 2-qt saucepan, over medium heat, melt butter. Use a wooden spoon to stir in flour. Gradually stir in milk. Reduce heat. Add cheese stirring constantly until cheese is melted. Add sauce. Remove from heat. Keep uncovered.

Steam pepper and onion 3 minutes. Add chard and steam 2 minutes longer.

Remove chard with tongs and spread on dinner dishes. Scatter macaroni on top. Pour sauce over both. Scatter pepper and onions over top. Sprinkle with seasoning.

OKRA, CHEESE, PASTA & "BACON"

½ cup uncooked ELBOW MACARONI

4 tbsp IMITATION BACON CHIPS

2 cups sliced OKRA

¾ cup SHARP CHEDDAR CHEESE

Follow directions on package to cook macaroni.

Pour ½ cup hot water over bacon chips. Set aside.

Steam okra 4 to 5 minutes.

Strain bacon chips. Combine all ingredients.

SERVES TWO

PASTA, SNOW PEAS & RED CABBAGE

½ cup ELBOW MACARONI

3 cups shredded RED CABBAGE

1½ cups sliced SNOW PEAS

3 pats BUTTER

½ can CREAM OF MUSHROOM
   SOUP

1/3 cup WATER

½ tsp CARAWAY SEED

Cook macaroni following directions on package.

Meantime steam cabbage 3 minutes. Add snow peas and steam 2 minutes longer.

Melt butter in a small saucepan and sauté mushrooms 3 minutes.

Remove steamer from pot. Cover vegetables to keep warm. Discard water. Add soup with 1/3 cup of water. Heat.

Add all ingredients. Simmer 1 minute.

PASTA, SNOW PEAS & RED PEPPER

½ cup uncooked ELBOW MACARONI

2 cups sliced SNOW PEAS

1 RED BELL PEPPER, halved, seeds
   removed, thinly sliced

3 pats BUTTER

1 GARLIC clove, minced

¾ cup WATER

½ cup chopped PARSLEY

1 EGG

2 tbsp ONION SOUP MIX

Cook macaroni following directions on package.

Meantime steam snow peas and pepper 2 minutes.

Melt butter in a large skillet. Sauté garlic 1 minute. Add water. Add egg and mix gently keeping yolk and white separate. Add parsley and onion soup mix. (Dump mix in small saucer. Mix ingredients evenly.)

Combine all ingredients in skillet. Simmer 1 minute.

SERVES TWO

PASTA, SPINACH & TOMATO

½ cup uncooked ELBOW MACARONI

1 cup sliced CHINESE PEAS

½ cup sliced MUSHROOMS

1 bunch SPINACH, stems removed,

½ can CREAM OF MUSHROOM SOUP

1/3 cup WATER

2 large, ripe TOMATOES, chopped small

2 tbsp minced CHIVES

1 tbsp chopped OREGANO leaves

Cook macaroni following directions on package.

After macaroni has been cooking a few minutes, steam chinese peas and mushrooms 3 minutes. Add spinach and steam 1 minute longer.

Remove steamer from pot. Cover vegetables to keep warm. Discard water. Add mushroom soup and water. Heat. Add remaining ingredients. Simmer 2 minutes.

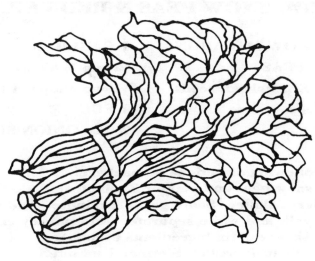

SERVES TWO

SPAGHETTI & SPINACH with PEPPERS

SPAGHETTI for two

1 RED BELL PEPPER, pulp and seeds
  removed, sliced in rings

1 tbsp BRAGG'S LIQUID AMINOS

1 tsp VIRGIN OLIVE OIL

1¼ cups chopped ZUCCHINI

2 GARLIC cloves, minced

3 tbsp WATER

2 pats BUTTER

1 or 2 tbsp grated PARMESAN
  CHEESE

1 lrg bunch SPINACH, stems removed

Cook spaghetti following directions on package.

Steam peppers 4 minutes in a large steamer.

Put aminos, oil, zucchini, and garlic in blender and liquefy. Transfer to small sauce pan. Put water in blender and swirl to remove residual zucchini. Add to sauce pan with butter and cheese. Simmer 2 minutes.

Add spinach to steamer and steam 1 minute.

Remove spinach with tongs and spread on dinner dishes. Layer spaghetti over top. Pour sauce over top. Place peppers on top.

PASTA & VEGETABLE SOUFFLÉ

½ cup uncooked ELBOW MACARONI

1 tsp SAFFLOWER OIL

3 pats BUTTER

¼ cup chopped ONION or SCALLION, sliced

2 cups MIX VEGETABLES

  CARROTS, sliced

  GREEN PEPPERS, chopped

  CELERY, slivered

STRING BEANS, sliced

1/3 cup WATER

1 package dry ONION SOUP

1 CORN cob, kerneled

½ cup grated CHEDDAR
  CHEESE

SERVES TWO

Cook macaroni following instructions on package.

When macaroni is almost done, heat oil and butter in a skillet. Sauté onion and mixed vegetables on medium-low 1 minute. Reduce heat. Sauté 2 minutes longer.

Add water and dry onion soup. Mix until blended. Turn off heat. Add macaroni and corn. Mix. Remove from heat. Mix in cheese.

SERVES TWO

BIBLIOGRAPHY

FIT FOR LIFE
    By Harry and Marilyn Diamond
    666 Fifth Avenue
    New York, NY 10103

THE HEALTH REPORTER
    (Series of 20 Volumes)
    Health Excellence Systems
    1108 Regal Row
    Manchaca, TX 78652

RECOMMENDED READING

Diet for a New America
by John Robbins
Earthsave
706 Fredrick Street
Santa Cruz, CA 95062

Pregnancy, Children & the Vegan Diet
By Michael Klaper, M.D.
Gentle World, Inc.
5425 Trilane Dr. S.W.
Atlanta, GA 30336

VEGETARIAN ORGANIZATIONS

VEGETARIAN SOCIETY INC.
PO Box 34427
Los Angeles, CA 90034
213-281-1907

VEGETARIAN AWARENESS NETWORK
PO Box 50515
Washington, DC 20004
800-USA-VEGE

AMERICAN VEGAN SOCIETY
PO Box H
Malaga, NJ 08328
609-694-2887

VEGETARIAN RESOURCE GROUP
PO Box 1463
Baltimore, MD 21203
301-366-VEGE

NORTH AMERICAN VEGETARIAN SOCIETY
PO Box 72
Dolgeville, NY 13329
518-568-7970

We spend the first half of our lives wasting our health to gain wealth. And the second half of our lives spending our wealth to regain our health. Author Unknown

Tell me what you eat and I'll tell you what you are. Anthelme Brilat-Savarin (1825)

We must eat to live, not live to eat. Fielding

Think of the fierce energy concentration in an acorn! You bury it in the ground, and it explodes into a great oak! Bury a sheep and nothing happens but decay. George Bernard Shaw

The Standard American Diet is a pathogenic arrangement that is responsible for a long list of diseases. This is evident when a mere change in diet enables SAD Sufferers to become free of their problems and lead healthful lives! T.C. Fry 1989.

Men dig their Graves with their own Teeth and die more by those fated Instruments than by the Weapons of their Enemies. Thomas Moffett, 1600.

We are the living graves of murdered beasts, slaughtered to satisfy our appetites. George Bernard Shaw, 1940.

It is my view that the vegetarian manner of living, by its purely physical effect on the human temperament, would most beneficially influence the lot of mankind. Albert Einstein, 1940.

It's great to let food be a pleasure! Just don't let food be your only treasure! Victoria Bid Well

Should a man, when ill, continue to eat the same amounts as when in health, he would surely die; while were he to eat more, he would surely die all the sooner. For his natural powers, already oppressed with sickness, would thereby be burdened with sickness, would thereby be burdened beyond endurance, having had forced upon them a quantity of food greater than they could support under the circumstances. A reduced quantity of food is, in my opinion, all that is required to sustain the individual into a long life. Luigi Coronado, 1458 - 1560.

Forbear, mortals, to pollute your bodies with the flesh of animals. There is corn; there are the apples that bear down the branches by their weight; and there are the grapes, nuts, and vegetables. These shall be our food. Pythagoras, 582 B.C.

Man is the only animal that must have as many as 30 different foods at one sitting. Dr. John Brosious, 1969.

A short life is not given us, but we ourselves make it so. Seneca, 62 A.D.

Scientists who have studied fasting have found that a forty year old man can be fasted for 3 weeks and be restored to the physiological level of a 17 year old! Now that is remarkable! Where else can you find anything which will restore youthfulness? There is nothing else in all the realm of nature that can accomplish this as can fasting. Dr. David J. Scott, 1980.

The secret to getting rid of old, destructive habits lies in loving and respecting yourself so much that you do not succumb to the addictive stimulation that is so powerfully projected to make us puppets on the strings of Madison Avenue manipulators.
Jo Willard, 1982.

Who is strong? He that can conquer bad habits! Ben Franklin, 1770

Habit is habit and not to be flung out the window by anyone...but coaxed down the stairs, one step at a time. Mark Twain, 1870.

But once we become aware of the impact of our food choices, we can never really forget. For the earth itself will remind us, as will our children and the animals and the forests and the sky and the rivers - that we are part of this earth, and it is part of us. All things are deeply connected, and so the choices we make in our daily lives have enormous influence, not only on our own health and vitality - but also on the lives of other beings, and indeed on the destiny of life on earth. John Robbins 1988.

It is a requisite that men and women should be content with little and accustom ourselves to eat no more than is absolutely necessary to support life - remember that all excess causes disease and leads to death. Luigi Coronado, 1458 - 1560.

Man lives on one-fourth of what he eats. On the other three-fourths lives his doctor. Inscription on an Egyptian pyramid, 3800 B.C.

The healthier you are, the easier it will be to control your thinking and recondition yourself to a sane way of living. The more physically healthy you become, the less effort it takes to control your emotions. The reverse is also true; the more control you have over your emotions, the more physically healthy you will become. It works both ways. Dr. Virginia Vetrano, 1988.

If you don't find time for exercise now, you will have to find time for illness later! Wayne Pickering, 1982.

What is impossible to see from the viewpoint of those who believe in "cures" is that the very symptoms the good doctors have suppressed and turned into chronic disease were the body's only means of correcting the problem! The so-called "disease" was the only "cure" possible. Dr. Phillip Chapman, 1981.

If the medical professionals courageously popularized the fast among their patients, there would be infinitely less suffering than there is now. That many would be saved who now die through the drug and feeding treatment is a certainty. Ghandi, 1945.

Behold! I have given you ever herb yielding seed, Which is upon the face of all the earth, and every tree, in which is the fruit of a tree yielding seed...To you, it shall be for food. God-In the Beginning

Physical, mental, and moral integrity constitute our most precious possessions - a balanced, sound mind in a balanced, sound body. We have a moral obligation to ourselves, dear ones, society, posterity, and our Maker to strive for optimum health through obedience to natural laws governing health. The physical, mental, and moral health of the people of any nation is more important than its "gross national product." Harry Kaplan, 1984.

The one sure road to better nutrition and better health is first to fast. Let your body do its professional and expert job of nourishing you during the fast, and then, with your taste buds cleansed of the false craving for junk, you will readily embrace the fresh fruits, vegetables, nuts and seeds and you can finally break away from the junk. Seneca, 62 A.D.

****

ORDER SHEET

THE GARDEN OF EDEN RAW FRUIT & VEGETABLE RECIPES - 120 pages ($10.95)
All vegan - no milk products.
Fruit Recipes - Hors D'Oeuvres, Fruit Dishes, Fruit Syrups, Fruit Shakes and Fruit Drinks.
Vegetable Recipes - Soups, Dips, Dressing (made from fresh vegetables - no vinegar, oil or mayonnaise), and Main Dishes.

THE 10-MINUTE VEGETARIAN COOK BOOK - 144 pages ($11.95)
All main dish recipes calling for fresh vegetables. All meals cook in 10 minutes or less.
Minimal use of processed foods.

STOP YOUR TINNITUS: Causes, Preventatives, Treatments ($14.95)
184 page book offers: External Causative Agents, Chemicals, Internal Causative Disorders, Physiological Intervention, Psychological Intervention, Alimentary Intervention, Telephone Hearing Screening Test, 13 pages of Glossary terms, 16 pages of Resources, 108 Medical and Scientific References.

The book shares the experiences of nine people from a Tinnitus Self-Help Group with the modalities that helped them stop their tinnitus.

Add $1.75 shipping for 1 book. $2.00 for 2 or 3. When shipped to California, add 8% sales tax. Please allow 3 to 4 weeks for delivery.

Order From:

Phyllis Avery
c/o Hygeia Publishing
1358 Fern Place
Vista, CA 92083